HAMMOND

ODYSSEY
ATLAS OF THE
World

Contents

ENTIRE CONTENTS
© COPYRIGHT MCMXCVI BY
HAMMOND INCORPORATED
All rights reserved. No part of this book may be reproduced or utilized in any form or by any means, electronic or mechanical, including photocopying, recording or by any information storage and retrieval system, without permission in writing from the Publisher. Printed in The United States of America.

LIBRARY OF CONGRESS
CATALOGING-IN-PUBLICATION DATA

Hammond Incorporated.
   Hammond odyssey atlas of the world.
     p. cm.
   Includes indexes.
   ISBN 0–8437–1188–4 (pbk.)
   1. Atlases. I.Title. II.Title:
Odyssey atlas of the world.
G1021.H27447   1994   <G&M>
912—dc20   93–48339
                  CIP
                  MAP

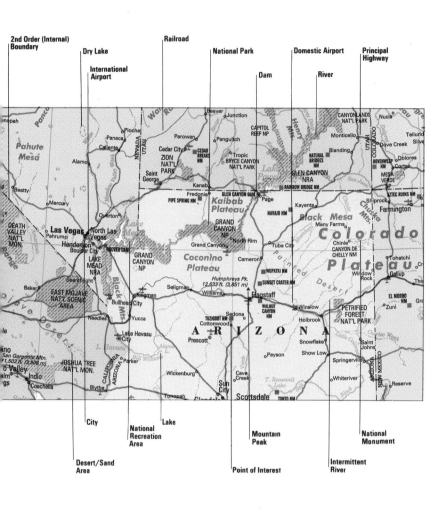

2nd Order (Internal) Boundary
Dry Lake
Railroad
National Park
Domestic Airport
Principal Highway
International Airport
Dam
River
City
National Recreation Area
Lake
Mountain Peak
National Monument
Desert/Sand Area
Point of Interest
Intermittent River

PRINCIPAL MAP ABBREVIATIONS

ABOR. RSV.	ABORIGINAL RESERVE	IND. RES.	INDIAN RESERVATION	NWR	NATIONAL WILDLIFE
ADMIN.	ADMINISTRATION	INT'L	INTERNATIONAL		RESERVE
AFB	AIR FORCE BASE	IR	INDIAN RESERVATION	OBL.	OBLAST
AMM. DEP.	AMMUNITION DEPOT	ISTH.	ISTHMUS	OCC.	OCCUPIED
ARCH.	ARCHIPELAGO	JCT.	JUNCTION	OKR.	OKRUG
ARPT.	AIRPORT	L.	LAKE	PAR.	PARISH
AUT.	AUTONOMOUS	LAG.	LAGOON	PASSG.	PASSAGE
B.	BAY	LAKESH.	LAKESHORE	PEN.	PENINSULA
BFLD.	BATTLEFIELD	MEM.	MEMORIAL	PK.	PEAK
BK.	BROOK	MIL.	MILITARY	PLAT.	PLATEAU
BOR.	BOROUGH	MISS.	MISSILE	PN	PARK NATIONAL
BR.	BRANCH	MON.	MONUMENT	PREF.	PREFECTURE
C.	CAPE	MT.	MOUNT	PROM.	PROMONTORY
CAN.	CANAL	MTN.	MOUNTAIN	PROV.	PROVINCE
CAP.	CAPITAL	MTS.	MOUNTAINS	PRSV.	PRESERVE
C.G.	COAST GUARD	NAT.	NATURAL	PT.	POINT
CHAN.	CHANNEL	NAT'L	NATIONAL	R.	RIVER
CO.	COUNTY	NAV.	NAVAL	RA	RECREATION AREA
CR.	CREEK	NB	NATIONAL	RA.	RANGE
CTR.	CENTER		BATTLEFIELD	REC.	RECREATION(AL)
DEP.	DEPOT	NBP	NATIONAL	REF.	REFUGE
DEPR.	DEPRESSION		BATTLEFIELD PARK	REG.	REGION
DEPT.	DEPARTMENT	NBS	NATIONAL	REP.	REPUBLIC
DES.	DESERT		BATTLEFIELD SITE	RES.	RESERVOIR,
DIST.	DISTRICT	NHP	NATIONAL HISTORICAL		RESERVATION
DMZ	DEMILITARIZED ZONE		PARK	RVWY.	RIVERWAY
DPCY.	DEPENDENCY	NHPP	NATIONAL HISTORICAL	SA.	SIERRA
ENG.	ENGINEERING		PARK AND PRESERVE	SD.	SOUND
EST.	ESTUARY	NHS	NATIONAL HISTORIC	SEASH.	SEASHORE
FD.	FIORD, FJORD		SITE	SO.	SOUTHERN
FED.	FEDERAL	NL	NATIONAL LAKESHORE	SP	STATE PARK
FK.	FORK	NM	NATIONAL MONUMENT	SPR., SPRS.	SPRING, SPRINGS
FLD.	FIELD	NMEMP	NATIONAL MEMORIAL	ST.	STATE
FOR.	FOREST		PARK	STA.	STATION
FT.	FORT	NMILP	NATIONAL MILITARY	STM.	STREAM
G.	GULF		PARK	STR.	STRAIT
GOV.	GOVERNOR	No.	NORTHERN	TERR.	TERRITORY
GOVT.	GOVERNMENT	NP	NATIONAL PARK	TUN.	TUNNEL
GD.	GRAND	NPP	NATIONAL PARK AND	TWP.	TOWNSHIP
GT.	GREAT		PRESERVE	VAL.	VALLEY
HAR.	HARBOR	NPRSV	NATIONAL PRESERVE	VILL.	VILLAGE
HD.	HEAD	NRA	NATIONAL	VOL.	VOLCANO
HIST.	HISTORIC(AL)		RECREATION AREA	WILD.	WILDLIFE,
HTS.	HEIGHTS	NRSV	NATIONAL RESERVE		WILDERNESS
I., IS.	ISLAND(S)	NS	NATIONAL SEASHORE	WTR.	WATER

PHYSICAL MAPS

The topography (relief) as well as the linework, colors and type for the continents and ocean floors is computer-generated and presents the relationships of land and sea forms with startling realism.

MAPS OF THE WORLD

These detailed regional maps are arranged by continent and introduced by physical and political maps of that continent which utilize Hammond's new Optimal Conformal projection.

On the regional maps, individual colors for each country highlight political divisions. A country's color remains the same on all regional maps. These maps also provide considerable information by locating numerous polit-ical and physical geographic features.

MASTER INDEX

This is an A-Z listing of names found on the political maps. It also has its own abbreviation list which, along with other Index keys, appears on page 65.

MAP SCALES

A map's scale is the relationship of any length on the map to an identical length on the earth's surface. A scale of 1:3,000,000 means that one inch on the map represents 3,000,000 inches (47 miles, 76 km.) on the earth's surface. A 1:1,000,000 scale (1/1) is larger than a 1:3,000,000 scale (1/3).

In this atlas, regional maps in Europe and North America are shown at scales of 1:7,000,000 and 1:10,500,000; Asia 1:10,500,000; South America 1:15,000,000; Africa 1:17,500,000; Australia 1:19,400,000.

In addition to these fractional scales, each map is accompanied by a linear scale for measuring distances (in miles and kilometers) on the map.

World Flags and Reference Guide

Afghanistan
Page/Location: 33/H2
Area: 250,775 sq. mi.
       649,507 sq. km.
Population: 16,450,000
Capital: Kabul
Largest City: Kabul
Highest Point: Noshaq
Monetary Unit: afghani

Albania
Page/Location: 21/H3
Area: 11,100 sq. mi.
       28,749 sq. km.
Population: 3,335,000
Capital: Tiranë
Largest City: Tiranë
Highest Point: Korab
Monetary Unit: lek

Algeria
Page/Location: 40/F2
Area: 919,591 sq. mi.
       2,381,740 sq. km.
Population: 26,022,000
Capital: Algiers
Largest City: Algiers
Highest Point: Tahat
Monetary Unit: Algerian dinar

Andorra
Page/Location: 20/D3
Area: 188 sq. mi.
       487 sq. km.
Population: 53,000
Capital: Andorra la Vella
Largest City: Andorra la Vella
Highest Point: Coma Pedrosa
Monetary Unit: Fr. franc, Sp. peseta

Angola
Page/Location: 42/C3
Area: 481,351 sq. mi.
       1,246,700 sq. km.
Population: 8,668,000
Capital: Luanda
Largest City: Luanda
Highest Point: Morro de Môco
Monetary Unit: kwanza

Antigua and Barbuda
Page/Location: 59/J4
Area: 171 sq. mi.
       443 sq. km.
Population: 64,000
Capital: St. John's
Largest City: St. John's
Highest Point: Boggy Peak
Monetary Unit: East Caribbean dollar

Argentina
Page/Location: 64/C4
Area: 1,072,070 sq. mi.
       2,776,661 sq. km.
Population: 32,664,000
Capital: Buenos Aires
Largest City: Buenos Aires
Highest Point: Cerro Aconcagua
Monetary Unit: Argentine peso

Armenia
Page/Location: 23/F5
Area: 11,506 sq. mi.
       29,800 sq. km.
Population: 3,283,000
Capital: Yerevan
Largest City: Yerevan
Highest Point: Alagez
Monetary Unit: Armenian ruble

Australia
Page/Location: 45
Area: 2,966,136 sq. mi.
       7,682,300 sq. km.
Population: 17,288,000
Capital: Canberra
Largest City: Sydney
Highest Point: Mt. Kosciusko
Monetary Unit: Australian dollar

Austria
Page/Location: 21/G2
Area: 32,375 sq. mi.
       83,851 sq. km.
Population: 7,666,000
Capital: Vienna
Largest City: Vienna
Highest Point: Grossglockner
Monetary Unit: schilling

Azerbaijan
Page/Location: 23/G5
Area: 33,436 sq. mi.
       86,600 sq. km.
Population: 7,029,000
Capital: Baku
Largest City: Baku
Highest Point: Bazardyuzyu
Monetary Unit: manat

Bahamas
Page/Location: 59/F2
Area: 5,382 sq. mi.
       13,939 sq. km.
Population: 252,000
Capital: Nassau
Largest City: Nassau
Highest Point: 207 ft. (63 m)
Monetary Unit: Bahamian dollar

Bahrain
Page/Location: 32/F3
Area: 240 sq. mi.
       622 sq. km.
Population: 537,000
Capital: Manama
Largest City: Manama
Highest Point: Jabal Dukhān
Monetary Unit: Bahraini dinar

Bangladesh
Page/Location: 34/E3
Area: 55,126 sq. mi.
       142,776 sq. km.
Population: 116,601,000
Capital: Dhaka
Largest City: Dhaka
Highest Point: Keokradong
Monetary Unit: taka

Barbados
Page/Location: 59/J5
Area: 166 sq. mi.
       430 sq. km.
Population: 255,000
Capital: Bridgetown
Largest City: Bridgetown
Highest Point: Mt. Hillaby
Monetary Unit: Barbadian dollar

Belarus
Page/Location: 19/L3
Area: 80,154 sq. mi.
       207,600 sq. km.
Population: 10,200,000
Capital: Minsk
Largest City: Minsk
Highest Point: Dzerzhinskaya
Monetary Unit: Belarusian ruble

Belgium
Page/Location: 18/E4
Area: 11,781 sq. mi.
       30,513 sq. km.
Population: 9,922,000
Capital: Brussels
Largest City: Brussels
Highest Point: Botrange
Monetary Unit: Belgian franc

Belize
Page/Location: 58/D4
Area: 8,867 sq. mi.
       22,966 sq. km.
Population: 228,000
Capital: Belmopan
Largest City: Belize City
Highest Point: Victoria Peak
Monetary Unit: Belize dollar

Benin
Page/Location: 40/F5
Area: 43,483 sq. mi.
       112,620 sq. km.
Population: 4,832,000
Capital: Porto-Novo
Largest City: Cotonou
Highest Point: Nassoukou
Monetary Unit: CFA franc

Bhutan
Page/Location: 34/E2
Area: 18,147 sq. mi.
       47,000 sq. km.
Population: 1,598,000
Capital: Thimphu
Largest City: Thimphu
Highest Point: Kula Kangri
Monetary Unit: ngultrum

Bolivia
Page/Location: 62/F7
Area: 424,163 sq. mi.
       1,098,582 sq. km.
Population: 7,157,000
Capital: La Paz; Sucre
Largest City: La Paz
Highest Point: Nevado Ancohuma
Monetary Unit: Bolivian peso

Bosnia and Herzegovina
Page/Location: 21/H2
Area: 19,940 sq. mi.
       51,645 sq. km.
Population: 4,124,256
Capital: Sarajevo
Largest City: Sarajevo
Highest Point: Maglič
Monetary Unit: —

Botswana
Page/Location: 42/D5
Area: 224,764 sq. mi.
       582,139 sq. km.
Population: 1,258,000
Capital: Gaborone
Largest City: Gaborone
Highest Point: Tsodilo Hills
Monetary Unit: pula

Brazil
Page/Location: 61/D3
Area: 3,284,426 sq. mi.
       8,506,663 sq. km.
Population: 155,356,000
Capital: Brasília
Largest City: São Paulo
Highest Point: Pico da Neblina
Monetary Unit: cruzeiro real

Brunei
Page/Location: 36/D2
Area: 2,226 sq. mi.
       5,765 sq. km.
Population: 398,000
Capital: Bandar Seri Begawan
Largest City: Bandar Seri Begawan
Highest Point: Bukit Pagon
Monetary Unit: Brunei dollar

Bulgaria
Page/Location: 21/K3
Area: 42,823 sq. mi.
       110,912 sq. km.
Population: 8,911,000
Capital: Sofia
Largest City: Sofia
Highest Point: Musala
Monetary Unit: lev

Burkina Faso
Page/Location: 40/E5
Area: 105,869 sq. mi.
       274,200 sq. km.
Population: 9,360,000
Capital: Ouagadougou
Largest City: Ouagadougou
Highest Point: 2,405 ft. (733 m)
Monetary Unit: CFA franc

Burma
Page/Location: 35/G3
Area: 261,789 sq. mi.
       678,034 sq. km.
Population: 42,112,000
Capital: Rangoon
Largest City: Rangoon
Highest Point: Hkakabo Razi
Monetary Unit: kyat

Burundi
Page/Location: 42/E1
Area: 10,747 sq. mi.
       27,835 sq. km.
Population: 5,831,000
Capital: Bujumbura
Largest City: Bujumbura
Highest Point: 8,760 ft. (2,670 m)
Monetary Unit: Burundi franc

Cambodia
Page/Location: 35/H5
Area: 69,898 sq. mi.
       181,036 sq. km.
Population: 7,146,000
Capital: Phnom Penh
Largest City: Phnom Penh
Highest Point: Phnum Aoral
Monetary Unit: riel

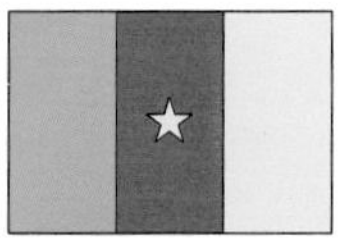

Cameroon
Page/Location: 42/H7
Area: 183,568 sq. mi.
475,441 sq. km.
Population: 11,390,000
Capital: Yaoundé
Largest City: Douala
Highest Point: Mt. Cameroon
Monetary Unit: CFA franc

Canada
Page/Location: 49/G4
Area: 3,851,787 sq. mi.
9,976,139 sq. km.
Population: 27,296,859
Capital: Ottawa
Largest City: Toronto
Highest Point: Mt. Logan
Monetary Unit: Canadian dollar

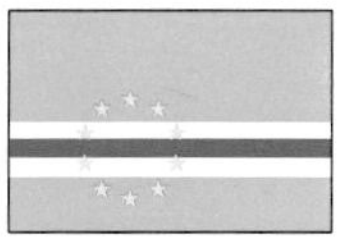

Cape Verde
Page/Location: 14/H5
Area: 1,557 sq. mi.
4,033 sq. km.
Population: 387,000
Capital: Praia
Largest City: Praia
Highest Point: 9,282 ft. (2,829 m)
Monetary Unit: Cape Verde escudo

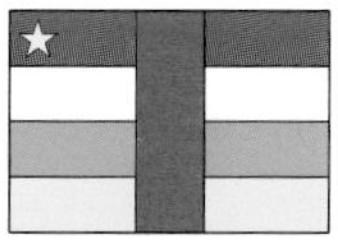

Central African Republic
Page/Location: 41/J6
Area: 242,000 sq. mi.
626,780 sq. km.
Population: 2,952,000
Capital: Bangui
Largest City: Bangui
Highest Point: Mt. Kayagangiri
Monetary Unit: CFA franc

Chad
Page/Location: 41/J4
Area: 495,752 sq. mi.
1,283,998 sq. km.
Population: 5,122,000
Capital: N'Djamena
Largest City: N'Djamena
Highest Point: Emi Koussi
Monetary Unit: CFA franc

Chile
Page/Location: 64/B3
Area: 292,257 sq. mi.
756,946 sq. km.
Population: 13,287,000
Capital: Santiago
Largest City: Santiago
Highest Point: Nevado Ojos del Salado
Monetary Unit: Chilean peso

China
Page/Location: 27/J6
Area: 3,691,000 sq. mi.
9,559,690 sq. km.
Population: 1,151,487,000
Capital: Beijing
Largest City: Shanghai
Highest Point: Mt. Everest
Monetary Unit: yuan

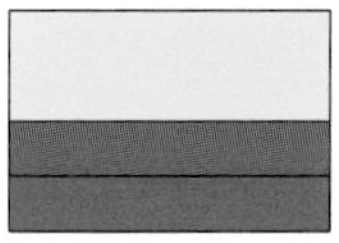

Colombia
Page/Location: 62/D3
Area: 439,513 sq. mi.
1,138,339 sq. km.
Population: 33,778,000
Capital: Bogotá
Largest City: Bogotá
Highest Point: Pico Cristóbal Colón
Monetary Unit: Colombian peso

Comoros
Page/Location: 39/G6
Area: 719 sq. mi.
1,862 sq. km.
Population: 477,000
Capital: Moroni
Largest City: Moroni
Highest Point: Karthala
Monetary Unit: Comorian franc

Congo
Page/Location: 80/D4
Area: 132,046 sq. mi.
342,000 sq. km.
Population: 2,309,000
Capital: Brazzaville
Largest City: Brazzaville
Highest Point: Lékéti Mts.
Monetary Unit: CFA franc

Costa Rica
Page/Location: 58/E5
Area: 19,575 sq. mi.
50,700 sq. km.
Population: 3,111,000
Capital: San José
Largest City: San José
Highest Point: Cerro Chirripó Grande
Monetary Unit: Costa Rican colón

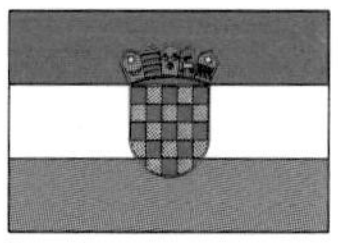

Croatia
Page/Location: 21/H2
Area: 22,050 sq. mi.
57,110 sq. km.
Population: 4,601,469
Capital: Zagreb
Largest City: Zagreb
Highest Point: Veliki Troglav
Monetary Unit: Croatian dinar

Cuba
Page/Location: 59/F3
Area: 44,206 sq. mi.
114,494 sq. km.
Population: 10,732,000
Capital: Havana
Largest City: Havana
Highest Point: Pico Turquino
Monetary Unit: Cuban peso

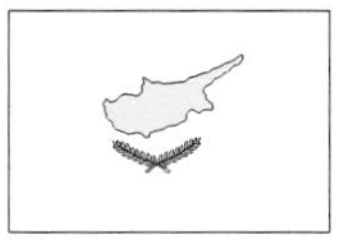

Cyprus
Page/Location: 32/B1
Area: 3,473 sq. mi.
8,995 sq. km.
Population: 709,000
Capital: Nicosia
Largest City: Nicosia
Highest Point: Olympus
Monetary Unit: Cypriot pound

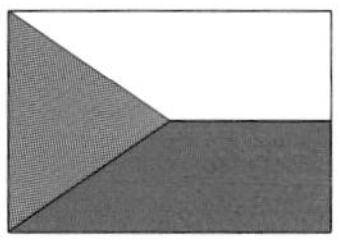

Czech Republic
Page/Location: 19/H4
Area: 30,449 sq. mi.
78,863 sq. km.
Population: 10,291,927
Capital: Prague
Largest City: Prague
Highest Point: Sněžka
Monetary Unit: Czech koruna

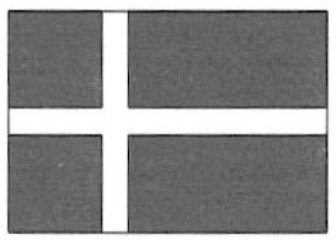

Denmark
Page/Location: 18/G3
Area: 16,629 sq. mi.
43,069 sq. km.
Population: 5,133,000
Capital: Copenhagen
Largest City: Copenhagen
Highest Point: Yding Skovhøj
Monetary Unit: Danish krone

Djibouti
Page/Location: 41/P5
Area: 8,880 sq. mi.
23,000 sq. km.
Population: 346,000
Capital: Djibouti
Largest City: Djibouti
Highest Point: Moussa Ali
Monetary Unit: Djibouti franc

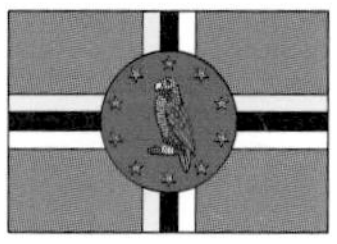

Dominica
Page/Location: 59/J4
Area: 290 sq. mi.
751 sq. km.
Population: 86,000
Capital: Roseau
Largest City: Roseau
Highest Point: Morne Diablotin
Monetary Unit: Dominican dollar

Dominican Republic
Page/Location: 59/H4
Area: 18,704 sq. mi.
48,443 sq. km.
Population: 7,385,000
Capital: Santo Domingo
Largest City: Santo Domingo
Highest Point: Pico Duarte
Monetary Unit: Dominican peso

Ecuador
Page/Location: 62/C4
Area: 109,483 sq. mi.
283,561 sq. km.
Population: 10,752,000
Capital: Quito
Largest City: Guayaquil
Highest Point: Chimborazo
Monetary Unit: sucre

Egypt
Page/Location: 41/L2
Area: 386,659 sq. mi.
1,001,447 sq. km.
Population: 54,452,000
Capital: Cairo
Largest City: Cairo
Highest Point: Mt. Catherine
Monetary Unit: Egyptian pound

El Salvador
Page/Location: 58/D5
Area: 8,260 sq. mi.
21,393 sq. km.
Population: 5,419,000
Capital: San Salvador
Largest City: San Salvador
Highest Point: Santa Ana
Monetary Unit: Salvadoran colón

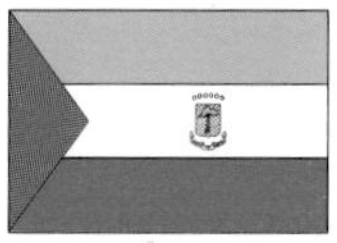

Equatorial Guinea
Page/Location: 40/G7
Area: 10,831 sq. mi.
28,052 sq. km.
Population: 379,000
Capital: Malabo
Largest City: Malabo
Highest Point: Pico de Santa Isabel
Monetary Unit: CFA franc

Eritrea
Page/Location: 41/N5
Area: 36,170 sq. mi.
93,679 sq. km.
Population: 3,500,000
Capital: Āsmera
Largest City: Āsmera
Highest Point: Soira
Monetary Unit: birr

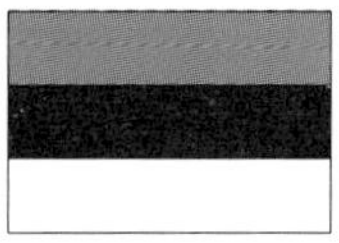

Estonia
Page/Location: 19/L2
Area: 17,413 sq. mi.
45,100 sq. km.
Population: 1,573,000
Capital: Tallinn
Largest City: Tallinn
Highest Point: Munamägi
Monetary Unit: kroon

Ethiopia
Page/Location: 41/N5
Area: 435,606 sq. mi.
1,128,220 sq. km.
Population: 51,617,000
Capital: Addis Ababa
Largest City: Addis Ababa
Highest Point: Ras Dashen Terara
Monetary Unit: birr

Fiji
Page/Location: 46/G6
Area: 7,055 sq. mi.
18,272 sq. km.
Population: 744,000
Capital: Suva
Largest City: Suva
Highest Point: Tomaniivi
Monetary Unit: Fijian dollar

Finland
Page/Location: 22/H2
Area: 130,128 sq. mi.
337,032 sq. km.
Population: 4,991,000
Capital: Helsinki
Largest City: Helsinki
Highest Point: Kahperusvaara
Monetary Unit: markka

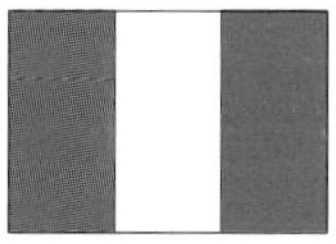

France
Page/Location: 20/D2
Area: 210,038 sq. mi.
543,998 sq. km.
Population: 58,073,553
Capital: Paris
Largest City: Paris
Highest Point: Mont Blanc
Monetary Unit: French franc

Gabon
Page/Location: 40/H7
Area: 103,346 sq. mi.
267,666 sq. km.
Population: 1,080,000
Capital: Libreville
Largest City: Libreville
Highest Point: Mt. Iboundji
Monetary Unit: CFA franc

Gambia
Page/Location: 40/B5
Area: 4,127 sq. mi.
10,689 sq. km.
Population: 875,000
Capital: Banjul
Largest City: Banjul
Highest Point: 98 ft. (30 m)
Monetary Unit: dalasi

Georgia
Page/Location: 23/F5
Area: 26,911 sq. mi.
69,700 sq. km.
Population: 5,449,000
Capital: Tbilisi
Largest City: Tbilisi
Highest Point: Kazbek
Monetary Unit: lari

Germany
Page/Location: 18/G4
Area: 137,753 sq. mi.
356,780 sq. km.
Population: 79,548,000
Capital: Berlin
Largest City: Berlin
Highest Point: Zugspitze
Monetary Unit: Deutsche mark

Ghana
Page/Location: 40/E6
Area: 92,099 sq. mi.
238,536 sq. km.
Population: 15,617,000
Capital: Accra
Largest City: Accra
Highest Point: Afadjoto
Monetary Unit: cedi

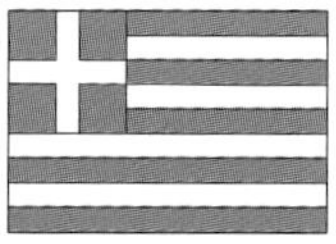

Greece
Page/Location: 21/J4
Area: 50,944 sq. mi.
131,945 sq. km.
Population: 10,043,000
Capital: Athens
Largest City: Athens
Highest Point: Mt. Olympus
Monetary Unit: drachma

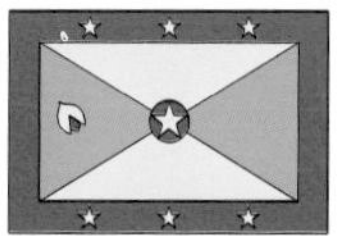

Grenada
Page/Location: 59/J5
Area: 133 sq. mi.
344 sq. km.
Population: 84,000
Capital: St. George's
Largest City: St. George's
Highest Point: Mt. St. Catherine
Monetary Unit: East Caribbean dollar

World Flags and Reference Guide

Guatemala
Page/Location: 58/C4
Area: 42,042 sq. mi.
108,889 sq. km.
Population: 9,266,000
Capital: Guatemala
Largest City: Guatemala
Highest Point: Tajumulco
Monetary Unit: quetzal

Guinea
Page/Location: 40/C5
Area: 94,925 sq. mi.
245,856 sq. km.
Population: 7,456,000
Capital: Conakry
Largest City: Conakry
Highest Point: Mt. Nimba
Monetary Unit: Guinea franc

Guinea-Bissau
Page/Location: 40/C5
Area: 13,948 sq. mi.
36,125 sq. km.
Population: 943,000
Capital: Bissau
Largest City: Bissau
Highest Point: 689 ft. (210 m)
Monetary Unit: Guinea-Bissau peso

Guyana
Page/Location: 62/G3
Area: 83,000 sq. mi.
214,970 sq. km.
Population: 1,024,000
Capital: Georgetown
Largest City: Georgetown
Highest Point: Mt. Roraima
Monetary Unit: Guyana dollar

Haiti
Page/Location: 59/G4
Area: 10,694 sq. mi.
27,697 sq. km.
Population: 6,287,000
Capital: Port-au-Prince
Largest City: Port-au-Prince
Highest Point: Pic la Selle
Monetary Unit: gourde

Honduras
Page/Location: 58/D4
Area: 43,277 sq. mi.
112,087 sq. km.
Population: 4,949,000
Capital: Tegucigalpa
Largest City: Tegucigalpa
Highest Point: Cerro de las Minas
Monetary Unit: lempira

Hungary
Page/Location: 21/H2
Area: 35,919 sq. mi.
93,030 sq. km.
Population: 10,558,000
Capital: Budapest
Largest City: Budapest
Highest Point: Kékes
Monetary Unit: forint

Iceland
Page/Location: 22/N7
Area: 39,768 sq. mi.
103,000 sq. km.
Population: 260,000
Capital: Reykjavík
Largest City: Reykjavík
Highest Point: Hvannadalshnúkur
Monetary Unit: króna

India
Page/Location: 34/C3
Area: 1,269,339 sq. mi.
3,287,588 sq. km.
Population: 869,515,000
Capital: New Delhi
Largest City: Calcutta
Highest Point: Nanda Devi
Monetary Unit: Indian rupee

Indonesia
Page/Location: 37/E4
Area: 788,430 sq. mi.
2,042,034 sq. km.
Population: 179,379,000
Capital: Jakarta
Largest City: Jakarta
Highest Point: Puncak Jaya
Monetary Unit: rupiah

Iran
Page/Location: 32/F2
Area: 636,293 sq. mi.
1,648,000 sq. km.
Population: 59,051,000
Capital: Tehran
Largest City: Tehran
Highest Point: Qolleh-ye Damāvand
Monetary Unit: Iranian rial

Iraq
Page/Location: 32/D2
Area: 172,476 sq. mi.
446,713 sq. km.
Population: 19,525,000
Capital: Baghdad
Largest City: Baghdad
Highest Point: Haji Ibrahim
Monetary Unit: Iraqi dinar

Ireland
Page/Location: 18/B3
Area: 27,136 sq. mi.
70,282 sq. km.
Population: 3,489,000
Capital: Dublin
Largest City: Dublin
Highest Point: Carrantuohill
Monetary Unit: Irish pound

Israel
Page/Location: 32/B2
Area: 7,847 sq. mi.
20,324 sq. km.
Population: 4,558,000
Capital: Jerusalem
Largest City: Tel Aviv-Yafo
Highest Point: Har Meron
Monetary Unit: shekel

Italy
Page/Location: 21/F3
Area: 116,303 sq. mi.
301,225 sq. km.
Population: 57,772,000
Capital: Rome
Largest City: Rome
Highest Point: Monte Rosa
Monetary Unit: Italian lira

Ivory Coast
Page/Location: 40/D6
Area: 124,504 sq. mi.
322,465 sq. km.
Population: 12,978,000
Capital: Yamoussoukro
Largest City: Abidjan
Highest Point: Mt. Nimba
Monetary Unit: CFA franc

Jamaica
Page/Location: 59/F4
Area: 4,411 sq. mi.
11,424 sq. km.
Population: 2,489,000
Capital: Kingston
Largest City: Kingston
Highest Point: Blue Mountain Pk.
Monetary Unit: Jamaican dollar

Japan
Page/Location: 29/M4
Area: 145,730 sq. mi.
377,441 sq. km.
Population: 124,017,000
Capital: Tokyo
Largest City: Tokyo
Highest Point: Fujiyama
Monetary Unit: yen

Jordan
Page/Location: 32/C2
Area: 35,000 sq. mi.
90,650 sq. km.
Population: 3,413,000
Capital: Amman
Largest City: Amman
Highest Point: Jabal Ramm
Monetary Unit: Jordanian dinar

Kazakhstan
Page/Location: 24/G5
Area: 1,048,300 sq. mi.
2,715,100 sq. km.
Population: 16,538,000
Capital: Alma-Ata
Largest City: Alma-Ata
Highest Point: Khan-Tengri
Monetary Unit: Kazakhstani ruble

Kenya
Page/Location: 41/N7
Area: 224,960 sq. mi.
582,646 sq. km.
Population: 25,242,000
Capital: Nairobi
Largest City: Nairobi
Highest Point: Mt. Kenya
Monetary Unit: Kenya shilling

Kiribati
Page/Location: 46/H5
Area: 291 sq. mi.
754 sq. km.
Population: 71,000
Capital: Bairiki
Largest City: —
Highest Point: Banaba Island
Monetary Unit: Australian dollar

Korea, North
Page/Location: 29/K3
Area: 46,540 sq. mi.
120,539 sq. km.
Population: 21,815,000
Capital: P'yŏngyang
Largest City: P'yŏngyang
Highest Point: Paektu-san
Monetary Unit: North Korean won

Korea, South
Page/Location: 29/K4
Area: 38,175 sq. mi.
98,873 sq. km.
Population: 43,134,000
Capital: Seoul
Largest City: Seoul
Highest Point: Halla-san
Monetary Unit: South Korean won

Kuwait
Page/Location: 32/E3
Area: 6,532 sq. mi.
16,918 sq. km.
Population: 2,204,000
Capital: Al Kuwait
Largest City: Al Kuwait
Highest Point: 951 ft. (290 m)
Monetary Unit: Kuwaiti dinar

Kyrgyzstan
Page/Location: 31/B3
Area: 76,641 sq. mi.
198,500 sq. km.
Population: 4,291,000
Capital: Bishkek
Largest City: Bishkek
Highest Point: Pik Pobedy
Monetary Unit: som

Laos
Page/Location: 35/H3
Area: 91,428 sq. mi.
236,800 sq. km.
Population: 4,113,000
Capital: Vientiane
Largest City: Vientiane
Highest Point: Phou Bia
Monetary Unit: kip

Latvia
Page/Location: 19/L2
Area: 24,595 sq. mi.
63,700 sq. km.
Population: 2,681,000
Capital: Riga
Largest City: Riga
Highest Point: Gaizina Kalns
Monetary Unit: lats

Lebanon
Page/Location: 32/C2
Area: 4,015 sq. mi.
10,399 sq. km.
Population: 3,385,000
Capital: Beirut
Largest City: Beirut
Highest Point: Qurnat as Sawdā'
Monetary Unit: Lebanese pound

Lesotho
Page/Location: 42/E6
Area: 11,720 sq. mi.
30,355 sq. km.
Population: 1,801,000
Capital: Maseru
Largest City: Maseru
Highest Point: Thabana-Ntlenyana
Monetary Unit: loti

Liberia
Page/Location: 40/D6
Area: 43,000 sq. mi.
111,370 sq. km.
Population: 2,973,000
Capital: Monrovia
Largest City: Monrovia
Highest Point: Mt. Wuteve
Monetary Unit: Liberian dollar

Libya
Page/Location: 41/J2
Area: 679,358 sq. mi.
1,759,537 sq. km.
Population: 5,057,000
Capital: Tripoli
Largest City: Tripoli
Highest Point: Picco Bette
Monetary Unit: Libyan dinar

Liechtenstein
Page/Location: 18/C5
Area: 61 sq. mi.
158 sq. km.
Population: 30,000
Capital: Vaduz
Largest City: Vaduz
Highest Point: Grauspitz
Monetary Unit: Swiss franc

Lithuania
Page/Location: 19/K3
Area: 25,174 sq. mi.
65,200 sq. km.
Population: 3,848,000
Capital: Vilnius
Largest City: Vilnius
Highest Point: Nevaišių
Monetary Unit: litas

Luxembourg
Page/Location: 18/F4
Area: 999 sq. mi.
2,587 sq. km.
Population: 402,000
Capital: Luxembourg
Largest City: Luxembourg
Highest Point: Ardennes Plateau
Monetary Unit: Luxembourg franc

Macedonia
Page/Location: 21/J3
Area: 9,889 sq. mi.
25,612 sq. km.
Population: 2,214,000
Capital: Skopje
Largest City: Skopje
Highest Point: Korab
Monetary Unit: denar

Madagascar
Page/Location: 42/K10
Area: 226,657 sq. mi.
587,041 sq. km.
Population: 13,428,000
Capital: Antananarivo
Largest City: Antananarivo
Highest Point: Maromokotro
Monetary Unit: Malagasy franc

Malawi
Page/Location: 42/F3
Area: 45,747 sq. mi.
118, 485 sq. km.
Population: 9,732,000
Capital: Lilongwe
Largest City: Blantyre
Highest Point: Mulanje Mts.
Monetary Unit: Malawi kwacha

Malaysia
Page/Location: 36/C2
Area: 128,308 sq. mi.
332,318 sq. km.
Population: 19,283,000
Capital: Kuala Lumpur
Largest City: Kuala Lumpur
Highest Point: Gunung Kinabalu
Monetary Unit: ringgit

Maldives
Page/Location: 27/G9
Area: 115 sq. mi.
298 sq. km.
Population: 252,000
Capital: Male
Largest City: Male
Highest Point: 20 ft. (6 m)
Monetary Unit: rufiyaa

Mali
Page/Location: 40/E4
Area: 464,873 sq. mi.
1,204,021 sq. km.
Population: 9,113,000
Capital: Bamako
Largest City: Bamako
Highest Point: Hombori Tondo
Monetary Unit: CFA franc

Malta
Page/Location: 21/G5
Area: 122 sq. mi.
316 sq. km.
Population: 367,000
Capital: Valletta
Largest City: Sliema
Highest Point: 830 ft. (253 m)
Monetary Unit: Maltese lira

Marshall Islands
Page/Location: 46/G3
Area: 70 sq. mi.
181 sq. km.
Population: 54,000
Capital: Majuro
Largest City: —
Highest Point: 20 ft. (6 m)
Monetary Unit: U.S. dollar

Mauritania
Page/Location: 40/C4
Area: 419,229 sq. mi.
1,085, 803 sq. km.
Population: 2,193,000
Capital: Nouakchott
Largest City: Nouakchott
Highest Point: Kediet Ijill
Monetary Unit: ouguiya

Mauritius
Page/Location: 15/M7
Area: 790 sq. mi.
2,046 sq. km.
Population: 1,117,000
Capital: Port Louis
Largest City: Port Louis
Highest Point: 2,713 ft. (827 m)
Monetary Unit: Mauritian rupee

Mexico
Page/Location: 58/A3
Area: 761,601 sq. mi.
1,972,546 sq. km.
Population: 92,202,000
Capital: Mexico City
Largest City: Mexico City
Highest Point: Citlaltépetl
Monetary Unit: Mexican peso

Micronesia
Page/Location: 46/D4
Area: 271 sq. mi.
702 sq. km.
Population: 120,347
Capital: Kolonia
Largest City: —
Highest Point: —
Monetary Unit: U.S. dollar

Moldova
Page/Location: 19/M5
Area: 13,012 sq. mi.
33,700 sq. km.
Population: 4,473,000
Capital: Chişinău
Largest City: Chişinău
Highest Point: 1,408 ft. (429 m)
Monetary Unit: leu

Monaco
Page/Location: 20/E3
Area: 368 acres
149 hectares
Population: 31,000
Capital: Monaco
Largest City: —
Highest Point: —
Monetary Unit: French franc

Mongolia
Page/Location: 28/D2
Area: 606,163 sq. mi.
1,569, 962 sq. km.
Population: 2,430,000
Capital: Ulaanbaatar
Largest City: Ulaanbaatar
Highest Point: Tavan Bogd Uul
Monetary Unit: tughrik

Morocco
Page/Location: 40/C1
Area: 172,414 sq. mi.
446,550 sq. km.
Population: 28,559,000
Capital: Rabat
Largest City: Casablanca
Highest Point: Jebel Toubkal
Monetary Unit: Moroccan dirham

Mozambique
Page/Location: 42/G4
Area: 303,769 sq. mi.
786,762 sq. km.
Population: 17,346,000
Capital: Maputo
Largest City: Maputo
Highest Point: Monte Binga
Monetary Unit: metical

Namibia
Page/Location: 42/C5
Area: 317,827 sq. mi.
823,172 sq. km.
Population: 1,596,000
Capital: Windhoek
Largest City: Windhoek
Highest Point: Brandberg
Monetary Unit: rand

Nauru
Page/Location: 46/F5
Area: 7.7 sq. mi.
20 sq. km.
Population: 10,000
Capital: Yaren (district)
Largest City: —
Highest Point: 230 ft. (70 m)
Monetary Unit: Australian dollar

Nepal
Page/Location: 34/D2
Area: 54,663 sq. mi.
141,577 sq. km.
Population: 21,042,000
Capital: Kāthmāndu
Largest City: Kāthmāndu
Highest Point: Mt. Everest
Monetary Unit: Nepalese rupee

Netherlands
Page/Location: 18/F3
Area: 15,892 sq. mi.
41,160 sq. km.
Population: 15,368,000
Capital: The Hague; Amsterdam
Largest City: Amsterdam
Highest Point: Vaalserberg
Monetary Unit: Netherlands guilder

New Zealand
Page/Location: 45/G6
Area: 103,736 sq. mi.
268,676 sq. km.
Population: 3,389,000
Capital: Wellington
Largest City: Auckland
Highest Point: Mt. Cook
Monetary Unit: New Zealand dollar

Nicaragua
Page/Location: 58/D5
Area: 45,698 sq. mi.
118,358 sq. km.
Population: 4,097,000
Capital: Managua
Largest City: Managua
Highest Point: Pico Mogotón
Monetary Unit: córdoba

Niger
Page/Location: 40/G4
Area: 489,189 sq. mi.
1,267,000 sq. km.
Population: 8,972,000
Capital: Niamey
Largest City: Niamey
Highest Point: Bagzane
Monetary Unit: CFA franc

Nigeria
Page/Location: 40/G6
Area: 357,000 sq. mi.
924,630 sq. km.
Population: 98,091,000
Capital: Abuja
Largest City: Lagos
Highest Point: Dimlang
Monetary Unit: naira

Norway
Page/Location: 22/C3
Area: 125,053 sq. mi.
323,887 sq. km.
Population: 4,315,000
Capital: Oslo
Largest City: Oslo
Highest Point: Glittertjnden
Monetary Unit: Norwegian krone

Oman
Page/Location: 33/G4
Area: 120,000 sq. mi.
310,800 sq. km.
Population: 1,701,000
Capital: Muscat
Largest City: Muscat
Highest Point: Jabal ash Shām
Monetary Unit: Omani rial

Pakistan
Page/Location: 33/H3
Area: 310,403 sq. mi.
803,944 sq. km.
Population: 128,856,000
Capital: Islāmābād
Largest City: Karāchi
Highest Point: K2 (Godwin Austen)
Monetary Unit: Pakistani rupee

Palau
Page/Location: 46/C4
Area: 177 sq. mi.
458 sq. km.
Population: 15,122
Capital: Koror
Largest City: Koror
Highest Point: 699 ft. (213m)
Monetary Unit: U.S. dollar

Panama
Page/Location: 58/E6
Area: 29,761 sq. mi.
77,082 sq. km.
Population: 2,630,000
Capital: Panamá
Largest City: Panamá
Highest Point: Barú
Monetary Unit: balboa

Papua New Guinea
Page/Location: 46/D5
Area: 183,540 sq. mi.
475,369 sq. km.
Population: 4,197,000
Capital: Port Moresby
Largest City: Port Moresby
Highest Point: Mt. Wilhelm
Monetary Unit: kina

World Flags and Reference Guide

Paraguay
Page/Location: 61/D5
Area: 157,047 sq. mi.
406,752 sq. km.
Population: 5,214,000
Capital: Asunción
Largest City: Asunción
Highest Point: Sierra de Amambay
Monetary Unit: guaraní

Peru
Page/Location: 62/C5
Area: 496,222 sq. mi.
1,285,215 sq. km.
Population: 23,651,000
Capital: Lima
Largest City: Lima
Highest Point: Nevado Huascarán
Monetary Unit: nuevo sol

Philippines
Page/Location: 30/D5
Area: 115,707 sq. mi.
299,681 sq. km.
Population: 69,809,000
Capital: Manila
Largest City: Manila
Highest Point: Mt. Apo
Monetary Unit: Philippine peso

Poland
Page/Location: 19/J3
Area: 120,725 sq. mi.
312,678 sq. km.
Population: 38,655,000
Capital: Warsaw
Largest City: Warsaw
Highest Point: Rysy
Monetary Unit: zloty

Portugal
Page/Location: 20/A4
Area: 35,549 sq. mi.
92,072 sq. km.
Population: 10,524,000
Capital: Lisbon
Largest City: Lisbon
Highest Point: Serra da Estrela
Monetary Unit: Portuguese escudo

Qatar
Page/Location: 32/F3
Area: 4,247 sq. mi.
11,000 sq. km.
Population: 513,000
Capital: Doha
Largest City: Doha
Highest Point: Dukhān Heights
Monetary Unit: Qatari riyal

Romania
Page/Location: 21/J2
Area: 91,699 sq. mi.
237,500 sq. km.
Population: 23,181,000
Capital: Bucharest
Largest City: Bucharest
Highest Point: Moldoveanul
Monetary Unit: leu

Russia
Page/Location: 24/H3
Area: 6,592,812 sq. mi.
17,075,400 sq. km.
Population: 149,609,000
Capital: Moscow
Largest City: Moscow
Highest Point: El'brus
Monetary Unit: Russian ruble

Rwanda
Page/Location: 42/E1
Area: 10,169 sq. mi.
26,337 sq. km.
Population: 8,374,000
Capital: Kigali
Largest City: Kigali
Highest Point: Karisimbi
Monetary Unit: Rwanda franc

Saint Kitts and Nevis
Page/Location: 59/J4
Area: 104 sq. mi.
269 sq. km.
Population: 41,000
Capital: Basseterre
Largest City: Basseterre
Highest Point: Mt. Misery
Monetary Unit: East Caribbean dollar

Saint Lucia
Page/Location: 59/J5
Area: 238 sq. mi.
616 sq. km.
Population: 145,000
Capital: Castries
Largest City: Castries
Highest Point: Mt. Gimie
Monetary Unit: East Caribbean dollar

Saint Vincent and the Grenadines
Page/Location: 59/J5
Area: 150 sq. mi.
388 sq. km.
Population: 115,000
Capital: Kingstown
Largest City: Kingstown
Highest Point: Soufrière
Monetary Unit: East Caribbean dollar

San Marino
Page/Location: 21/G3
Area: 23.4 sq. mi.
60.6 sq. km.
Population: 24,000
Capital: San Marino
Largest City: San Marino
Highest Point: Monte Titano
Monetary Unit: Italian lira

São Tomé and Príncipe
Page/Location: 40/G7
Area: 372 sq. mi.
963 sq. km.
Population: 137,000
Capital: São Tomé
Largest City: São Tomé
Highest Point: Pico de São Tomé
Monetary Unit: dobra

Saudi Arabia
Page/Location: 32/D4
Area: 829,995 sq. mi.
2,149,687 sq. km.
Population: 18,197,000
Capital: Riyadh
Largest City: Riyadh
Highest Point: Jabal Sawdā'
Monetary Unit: Saudi riyal

Senegal
Page/Location: 40/C5
Area: 75,954 sq. mi.
196,720 sq. km.
Population: 8,731,000
Capital: Dakar
Largest City: Dakar
Highest Point: Fouta Djallon
Monetary Unit: CFA franc

Seychelles
Page/Location: 15/M6
Area: 145 sq. mi.
375 sq. km.
Population: 72,000
Capital: Victoria
Largest City: Victoria
Highest Point: Morne Seychellois
Monetary Unit: Seychellois rupee

Sierra Leone
Page/Location: 40/C6
Area: 27,925 sq. mi.
72,325 sq. km.
Population: 4,630,000
Capital: Freetown
Largest City: Freetown
Highest Point: Loma Mansa
Monetary Unit: leone

Singapore
Page/Location: 36/B3
Area: 226 sq. mi.
585 sq. km.
Population: 2,859,000
Capital: Singapore
Largest City: Singapore
Highest Point: Bukit Timah
Monetary Unit: Singapore dollar

Slovakia
Page/Location: 19/J4
Area: 18,924 sq. mi.
49,013 sq. km.
Population: 5,404,000
Capital: Bratislava
Largest City: Bratislava
Highest Point: Gerlachovský Štít
Monetary Unit: Slovak koruna

Slovenia
Page/Location: 21/G2
Area: 7,898 sq mi.
20,456 sq. km.
Population: 1,972,000
Capital: Ljubljana
Largest City: Ljubljana
Highest Point: Triglav
Monetary Unit: tolar

Solomon Islands
Page/Location: 46/E6
Area: 11,500 sq. mi.
29,785 sq. km.
Population: 386,000
Capital: Honiara
Largest City: Honiara
Highest Point: Mt. Makarakomburu
Monetary Unit: Solomon Islands dollar

Somalia
Page/Location: 41/Q6
Area: 246,200 sq. mi.
637,658 sq. km.
Population: 6,667,000
Capital: Mogadishu
Largest City: Mogadishu
Highest Point: Shimber Berris
Monetary Unit: Somali shilling

South Africa
Page/Location: 42/D6
Area: 455,318 sq. mi.
1,179,274 sq. km.
Population: 43,931,000
Capital: Cape Town; Pretoria
Largest City: Johannesburg
Highest Point: Injasuti
Monetary Unit: rand

Spain
Page/Location: 20/B3
Area: 194,881 sq. mi.
504,742 sq. km.
Population: 39,303,000
Capital: Madrid
Largest City: Madrid
Highest Point: Pico de Teide
Monetary Unit: peseta

Sri Lanka
Page/Location: 34/D6
Area: 25,332 sq. mi.
65,610 sq. km.
Population: 18,130,000
Capital: Colombo
Largest City: Colombo
Highest Point: Pidurutalagala
Monetary Unit: Sri Lanka rupee

Sudan
Page/Location: 41/L5
Area: 967,494 sq. mi.
2,505,809 sq. km.
Population: 29,420,000
Capital: Khartoum
Largest City: Omdurman
Highest Point: Jabal Marrah
Monetary Unit: Sudanese pound

Suriname
Page/Location: 63/G3
Area: 55,144 sq. mi.
142,823 sq. km.
Population: 423,000
Capital: Paramaribo
Largest City: Paramaribo
Highest Point: Juliana Top
Monetary Unit: Suriname guilder

Swaziland
Page/Location: 42/F6
Area: 6,705 sq. mi.
17,366 sq. km.
Population: 936,000
Capital: Mbabane
Largest City: Mbabane
Highest Point: Emlembe
Monetary Unit: lilangeni

Sweden
Page/Location: 22/E3
Area: 173,665 sq. mi.
449,792 sq. km.
Population: 8,778,000
Capital: Stockholm
Largest City: Stockholm
Highest Point: Kebnekaise
Monetary Unit: krona

Switzerland
Page/Location: 20/E2
Area: 15,943 sq. mi.
41,292 sq. km.
Population: 7,040,000
Capital: Bern
Largest City: Zürich
Highest Point: Dufourspitze
Monetary Unit: Swiss franc

Syria
Page/Location: 32/C1
Area: 71,498 sq. mi.
185,180 sq. km.
Population: 14,887,000
Capital: Damascus
Largest City: Damascus
Highest Point: Jabal ash Shaykh
Monetary Unit: Syrian pound

Taiwan
Page/Location: 30/D3
Area: 13,971 sq. mi.
36,185 sq. km.
Population: 21,299,000
Capital: Taipei
Largest City: Taipei
Highest Point: Yü Shan
Monetary Unit: new Taiwan dollar

Tajikistan
Page/Location: 24/H6
Area: 55,251 sq. mi.
143,100 sq. km.
Population: 5,995,000
Capital: Dushanbe
Largest City: Dushanbe
Highest Point: Communism Peak
Monetary Unit: Tajik ruble

Tanzania
Page/Location: 42/F2
Area: 363,708 sq. mi.
942,003 sq. km.
Population: 27,986,000
Capital: Dar es Salaam
Largest City: Dar es Salaam
Highest Point: Kilimanjaro
Monetary Unit: Tanzanian shilling

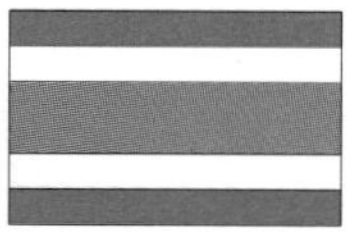

Thailand
Page/Location: 35/H4
Area: 198,455 sq. mi.
513,998 sq. km.
Population: 59,510,000
Capital: Bangkok
Largest City: Bangkok
Highest Point: Doi Inthanon
Monetary Unit: baht

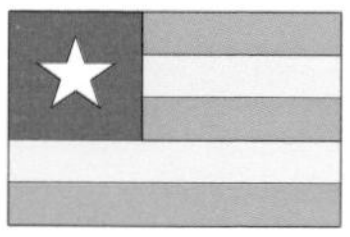

Togo
Page/Location: 40/F6
Area: 21,622 sq. mi.
56,000 sq. km.
Population: 4,255,000
Capital: Lomé
Largest City: Lomé
Highest Point: Mt. Agou
Monetary Unit: CFA franc

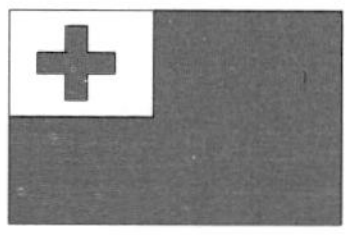

Tonga
Page/Location: 47/H7
Area: 270 sq. mi.
699 sq. km.
Population: 105,000
Capital: Nuku'alofa
Largest City: Nuku'alofa
Highest Point: Kao Island
Monetary Unit: pa'anga

Trinidad and Tobago
Page/Location: 58/J5
Area: 1,980 sq. mi.
5,128 sq. km.
Population: 1,328,000
Capital: Port-of-Spain
Largest City: Port-of-Spain
Highest Point: El Cerro del Aripo
Monetary Unit: Trin. & Tobago dollar

Tunisia
Page/Location: 40/G1
Area: 63,378 sq. mi.
164,149 sq. km.
Population: 8,727,000
Capital: Tūnis
Largest City: Tūnis
Highest Point: Jabal ash Sha'nabī
Monetary Unit: Tunisian dinar

Turkey
Page/Location: 23/D6
Area: 300,946 sq. mi.
779,450 sq. km.
Population: 62,154,000
Capital: Ankara
Largest City: Istanbul
Highest Point: Mt. Ararat
Monetary Unit: Turkish lira

Turkmenistan
Page/Location: 24/F6
Area: 188,455 sq. mi.
488,100 sq. km.
Population: 3,995,000
Capital: Ashkhabad
Largest City: Ashkhabad
Highest Point: Rize
Monetary Unit: manat

Tuvalu
Page/Location: 46/G5
Area: 9.78 sq. mi.
25.33 sq. km.
Population: 10,000
Capital: Funafuti
Largest City: —
Highest Point: 16 ft. (5 m)
Monetary Unit: Australian dollar

Uganda
Page/Location: 41/M7
Area: 91,076 sq. mi.
235,887 sq. km.
Population: 19,859,000
Capital: Kampala
Largest City: Kampala
Highest Point: Margherita Peak
Monetary Unit: Ugandan shilling

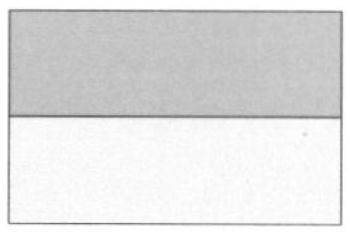

Ukraine
Page/Location: 23/C4
Area: 233,089 sq. mi.
603,700 sq. km.
Population: 51,847,000
Capital: Kiev
Largest City: Kiev
Highest Point: Goverla
Monetary Unit: karbovanet

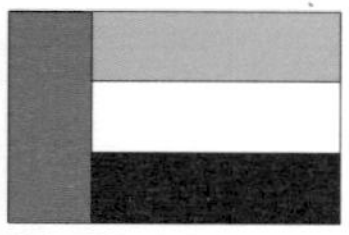

United Arab Emirates
Page/Location: 32/F4
Area: 32,278 sq. mi.
83,600 sq. km.
Population: 2,791,000
Capital: Abu Dhabi
Largest City: Dubayy
Highest Point: Hajar Mts.
Monetary Unit: Emirian dirham

United Kingdom
Page/Location: 18/D3
Area: 94,399 sq. mi.
244,493 sq. km.
Population: 58,135,000
Capital: London
Largest City: London
Highest Point: Ben Nevis
Monetary Unit: pound sterling

United States
Page/Location: 49/G5
Area: 3,540,542 sq. mi.
9,170,002 sq. km.
Population: 260,714,000
Capital: Washington
Largest City: New York
Highest Point: Mt. McKinley
Monetary Unit: U.S. dollar

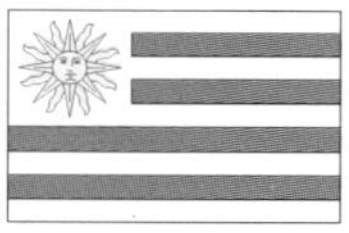

Uruguay
Page/Location: 64/E3
Area: 72,172 sq. mi.
186,925 sq. km.
Population: 3,199,000
Capital: Montevideo
Largest City: Montevideo
Highest Point: Cerro Catedral
Monetary Unit: Uruguayan peso

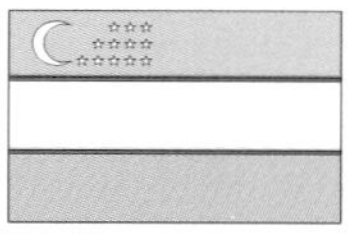

Uzbekistan
Page/Location: 24/G5
Area: 173,591 sq. mi.
449,600 sq. km.
Population: 22,609,000
Capital: Tashkent
Largest City: Tashkent
Highest Point: Khodzha-Pir'yakh
Monetary Unit: som

Vanuatu
Page/Location: 46/F6
Area: 5,700 sq. mi.
14,763 sq. km.
Population: 170,000
Capital: Vila
Largest City: Vila
Highest Point: Tabwemasana
Monetary Unit: vatu

Vatican City
Page/Location: 21/G3
Area: 108.7 acres
44 hectares
Population: 821
Capital: —
Largest City: —
Highest Point: —
Monetary Unit: Italian lira

Venezuela
Page/Location: 62/E2
Area: 352,143 sq. mi.
912,050 sq. km.
Population: 20,562,000
Capital: Caracas
Largest City: Caracas
Highest Point: Pico Bolívar
Monetary Unit: bolívar

Vietnam
Page/Location: 35/J5
Area: 128,405 sq. mi.
332,569 sq. km.
Population: 73,104,000
Capital: Hanoi
Largest City: Ho Chi Minh City
Highest Point: Fan Si Pan
Monetary Unit: dong

Western Samoa
Page/Location: 47/H6
Area: 1,133 sq. mi.
2,934 sq. km.
Population: 204,000
Capital: Apia
Largest City: Apia
Highest Point: Mt. Silisili
Monetary Unit: tala

Yemen
Page/Location: 32/E5
Area: 188,321 sq. mi.
487,752 sq. km.
Population: 11,105,000
Capital: Sanaa
Largest City: Aden
Highest Point: Nabī Shu'ayb
Monetary Unit: Yemeni rial

Yugoslavia
Page/Location: 21/J3
Area: 38,989 sq. mi.
100,982 sq. km.
Population: 10,760,000
Capital: Belgrade
Largest City: Belgrade
Highest Point: Đaravica
Monetary Unit: Yugoslav new dinar

Zaire
Page/Location: 39/E5
Area: 905,063 sq. mi.
2,344,113 sq. km.
Population: 42,684,000
Capital: Kinshasa
Largest City: Kinshasa
Highest Point: Margherita Peak
Monetary Unit: zaire

Zambia
Page/Location: 42/E3
Area: 290,586 sq. mi.
752,618 sq. km.
Population: 9,188,000
Capital: Lusaka
Largest City: Lusaka
Highest Point: Sunzu
Monetary Unit: Zambian kwacha

Zimbabwe
Page/Location: 42/E4
Area: 150,803 sq. mi.
390,580 sq. km.
Population: 10,975,000
Capital: Harare
Largest City: Harare
Highest Point: Inyangani
Monetary Unit: Zimbabwe dollar

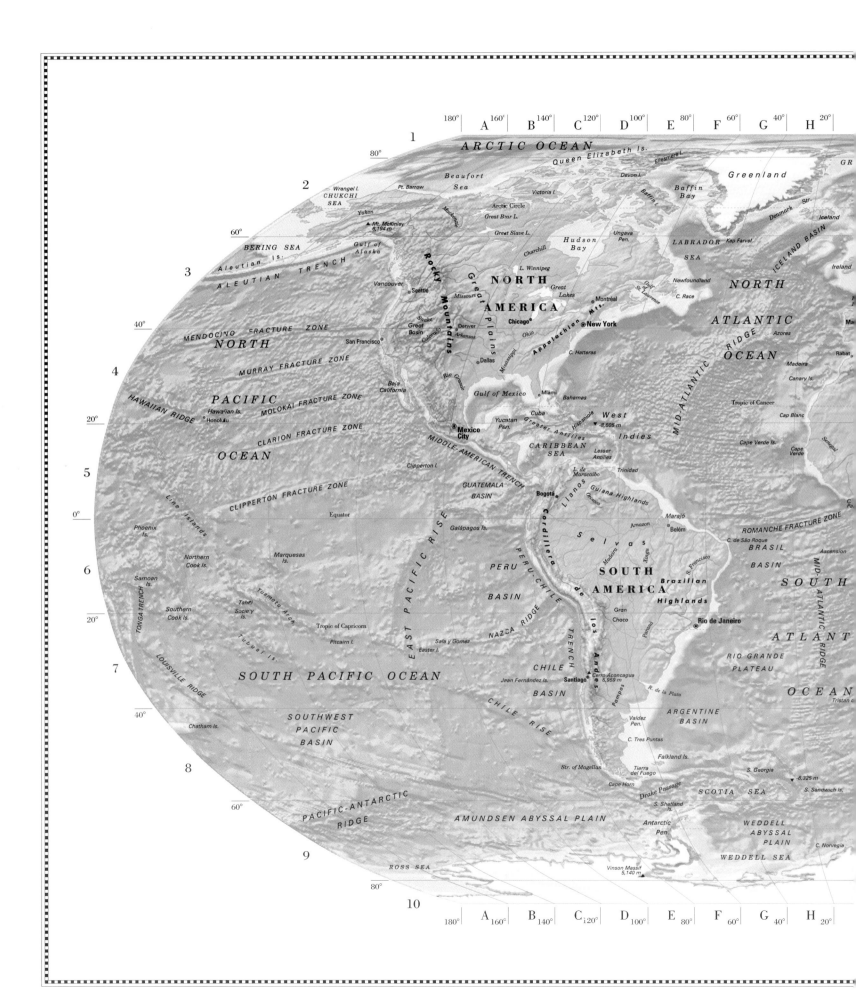

World - Physical

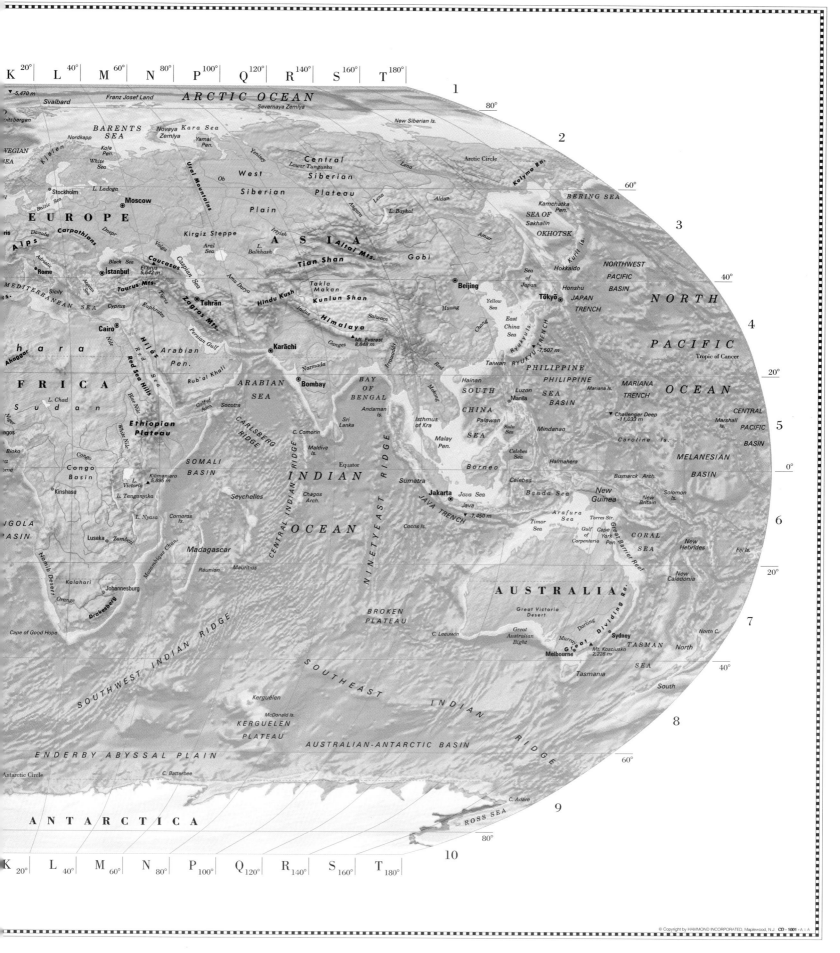

K 20° **L** 40° **M** 60° **N** 80° **P** 100° **Q** 120° **R** 140° **S** 160° **T** 180°

1

2

3

4

5

6

7

8

9

10

ARCTIC OCEAN

80°

▼ -5,470 m
Svalbard
Franz Josef Land
Severnaya Zemlya
New Siberian Is.
Arctic Circle

Spitsbergen
BARENTS SEA
Nordkapp
Novaya Zemlya
Kara Sea
Yamal Pen.

NEGIAN SEA
Kjølen
Kola Pen.
White Sea
Ob
Yenisey
Lower Tunguska
Central Siberian Plateau
Lena
Kolyma Ra.
60°
BERING SEA

Stockholm
L. Ladoga
West Siberian Plain
Angara
Aldan
Kamchatka Pen.

Baltic Sea
Moscow
Irtysh
L. Baykal
Amur
SEA OF OKHOTSK
Sakhalin

EUROPE
Dnepr
Kirgiz Steppe
ASIA
Altai Mts.
Gobi
Sea of Japan
Hokkaido
NORTHWEST PACIFIC BASIN
40°

Alps
Carpathians
Danube
Volga
Aral Sea
Balkhash
Tian Shan
Beijing
Huang
Yellow Sea
Tōkyō
Honshu
JAPAN TRENCH
NORTH

Adriatic
Rome
İstanbul
Black Sea
Caucasus
El'brus 5,642 m
Caspian Sea
Amu Darya
Takla Makan
Kunlun Shan
Chang
East China Sea
Ryukyu Is.
RYUKYU TRENCH
▼ -7,507 m
PACIFIC

Sicily
Aegean Sea
Taurus Mts.
Zagros Mts.
Tehrān
Hindu Kush
Himalaya
Saluween
Mt. Everest 8,848 m
Taiwan
PHILIPPINE
MARIANA TRENCH
OCEAN
Tropic of Cancer

MEDITERRANEAN SEA
Cyprus
Euphrates
Tigris
Persian Gulf
Indus
Ganges
Narmada
Red
Hainan
PHILIPPINE SEA BASIN
Mariana Is.
20°

Cairo
Nile
Hilâl
Arabian Pen.
Karāchi
ARABIAN SEA
Bombay
BAY OF BENGAL
SOUTH CHINA SEA
Luzon
Manila
MARSHALL
CENTRAL PACIFIC BASIN

hara
Ahaggar
Red Sea Hills
Rub' al Khali
C. Comorin
Sri Lanka
Andaman
Isthmus of Kra
Palawan
Mindanao
Challenger Deep -11,033 m
Caroline Is.

FRICA
Sudan
L. Chad
Blue Nile
Ethiopian Plateau
CARLSBERG RIDGE
Maldive Is.
Malay Pen.
Sulu Sea
Celebes Sea
MELANESIAN BASIN
5

Niger
Bioko
White Nile
SOMALI BASIN
Seychelles
Chagos Arch.
Equator
Sumatra
Borneo
Celebes
Halmahera
Bismarck Arch.
0°

Lagos
Congo
Congo Basin
Kinshasa
L. Victoria
Kilimanjaro 5,895 m
L. Tanganyika
CENTRAL INDIAN RIDGE
INDIAN
Jakarta
Java Sea
Banda Sea
New Guinea
New Britain
Solomon Is.

NGOLA
ASIN
L. Nyasa
Comoros Is.
Java
JAVA TRENCH
▼ -7,450 m
Arafura Sea
Cape York Pen.
CORAL SEA
New Hebrides
Fiji Is.
6

Lusaka
Zambezi
Madagascar
Réunion
Mauritius
OCEAN
Cocos Is.
Timor Sea
Gulf of Carpentaria
Great Barrier Reef
20°

Namib Desert
Orange
Kalahari
Johannesburg
Mozambique Chan.
NINETYEAST RIDGE
AUSTRALIA
Great Victoria Desert
New Caledonia

Drakensberg
Cape of Good Hope
SOUTHWEST INDIAN RIDGE
BROKEN PLATEAU
C. Leeuwin
Great Australian Bight
Murray
Darling
Great Dividing Ra.
Sydney
TASMAN
North C.
7

SOUTHEAST
Melbourne
Mt. Kosciusko 2,228 m
SEA
North
40°

Kerguélen
INDIAN RIDGE
Tasmania
South

McDonald Is.
KERGUELEN PLATEAU
AUSTRALIAN-ANTARCTIC BASIN
8

ENDERBY ABYSSAL PLAIN
60°

Antarctic Circle
C. Batterbee
C. Adare
9

ANTARCTICA
ROSS SEA
80°
10

K 20° **L** 40° **M** 60° **N** 80° **P** 100° **Q** 120° **R** 140° **S** 160° **T** 180°

POPULATION OF CITIES AND TOWNS

⊕ OVER 5,000,000   ⊙ 500,000 - 1,999,999
◉ 2,000,000 - 4,999,999   ○ UNDER 500,000

SCALE 1:81,700,000   ROBINSON PROJECTION   STANDARD PARALLELS 38°N AND 38°S

MILES 0 ___ 1000 ___ 2000 ___ 3000 ___ 4000
KILOMETERS 0 ___ 1000 ___ 2000 ___ 3000 ___ 4000

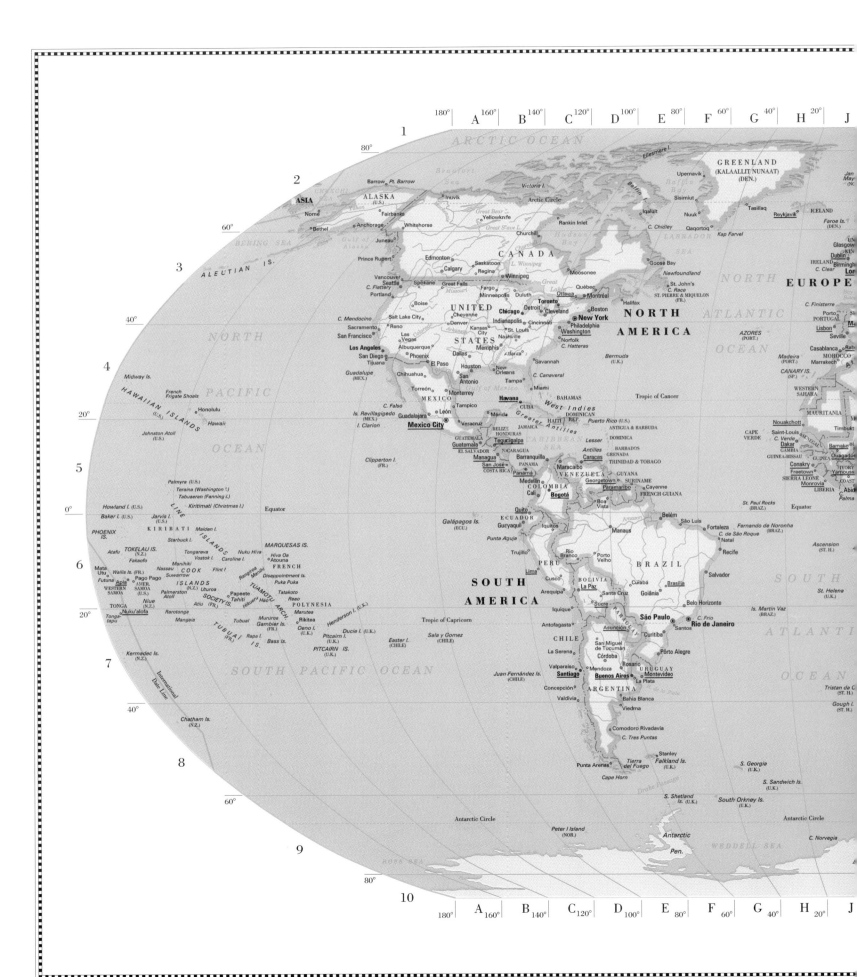

World - Political

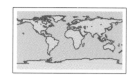

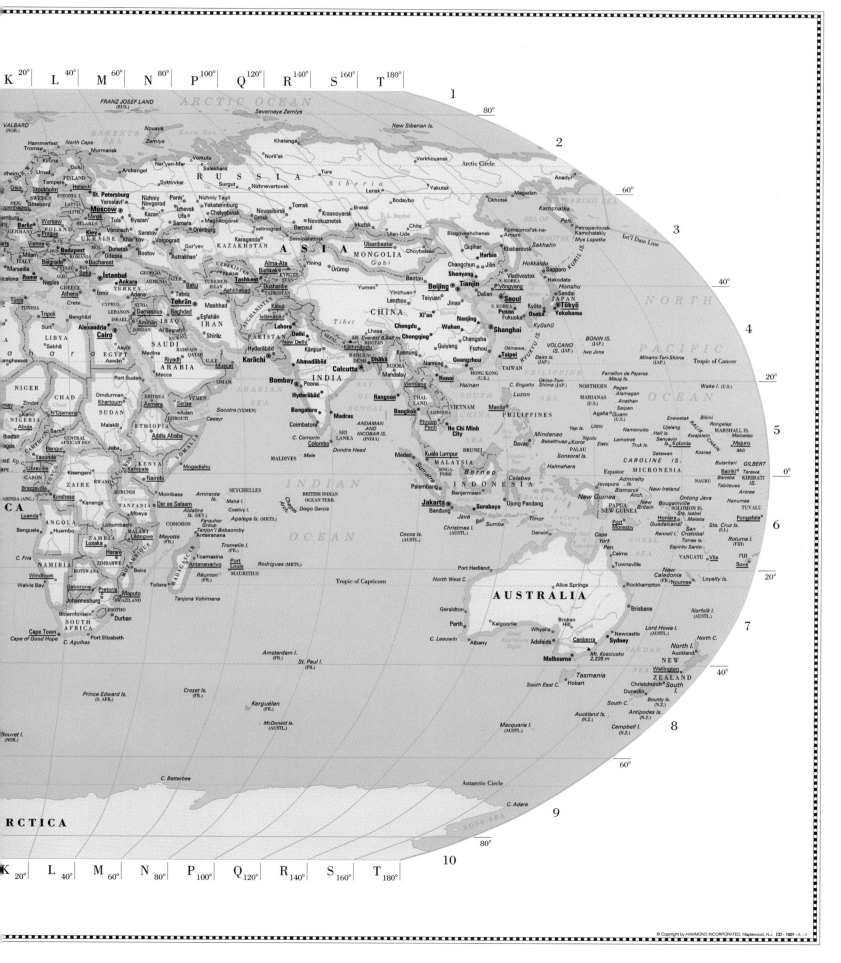

POPULATION OF CITIES AND TOWNS
- ◉ OVER 5,000,000
- ● 2,000,000 - 4,999,999
- ● 500,000 - 1,999,999
- ○ UNDER 500,000

SCALE 1:81,700,000   ROBINSON PROJECTION   STANDARD PARALLELS 38°N AND 38°S

MILES 0 — 1000 — 2000 — 3000 — 4000
KILOMETERS 0 — 1000 — 2000 — 3000 — 4000

© Copyright by HAMMOND INCORPORATED, Maplewood, N.J. CD - 1001 - A-A

Europe - Physical

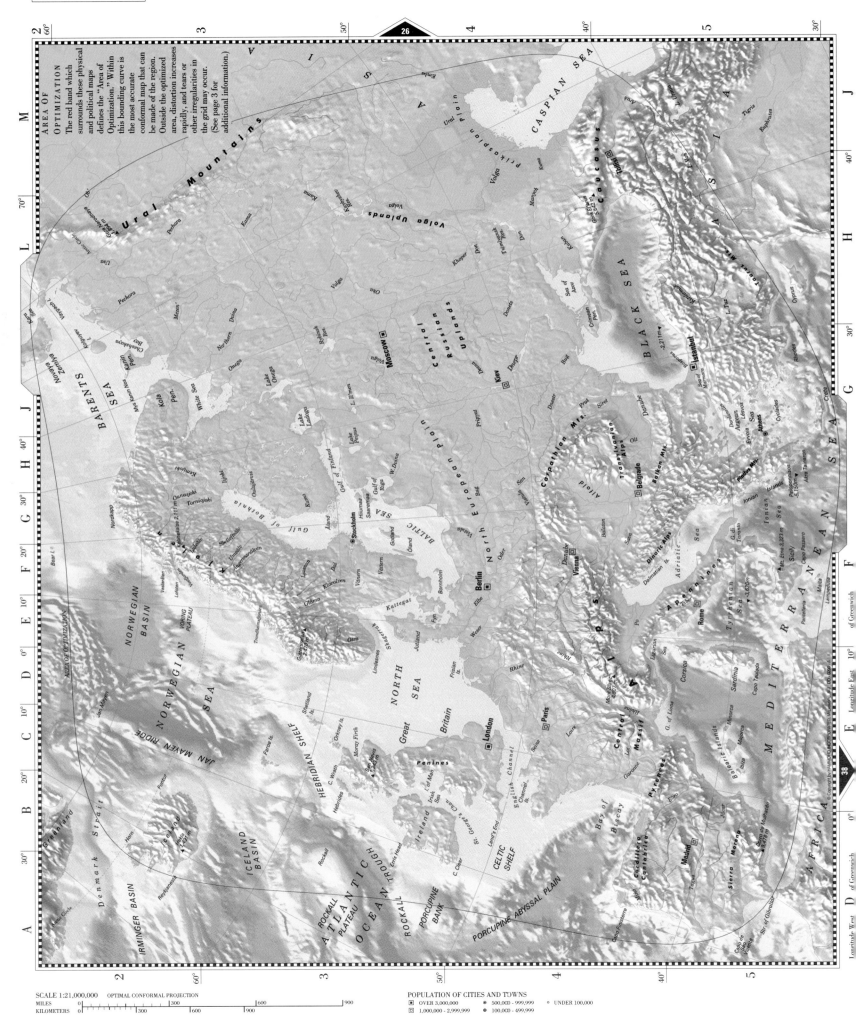

AREA OF OPTIMIZATION
The red band which surrounds these physical and political maps defines the "Area of Optimization." Within this bounding curve is the most accurate conformal map that can be made of the region. Outside the optimized area, distortion increases rapidly, and tears or other irregularities in the grid may occur. (See page 3 for additional information.)

SCALE 1:21,000,000   OPTIMAL CONFORMAL PROJECTION

MILES   0   300   600   900

KILOMETERS 0   300   600   900

POPULATION OF CITIES AND TOWNS

▣ OVER 3,000,000   ⊛ 500,000 - 999,999   ○ UNDER 100,000
▣ 1,000,000 - 2,999,999   ⊛ 100,000 - 499,999

Europe - Political

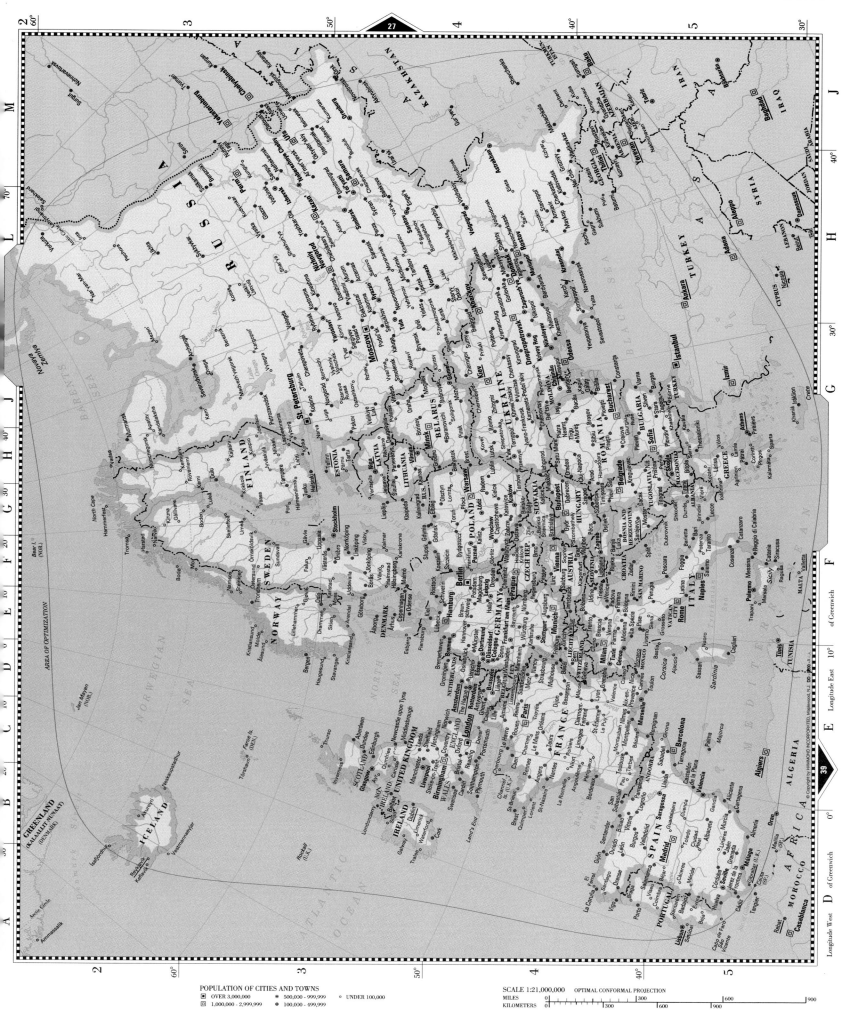

POPULATION OF CITIES AND TOWNS

- ▣ OVER 3,000,000
- ◉ 500,000 - 999,999
- ○ UNDER 100,000
- ▣ 1,000,000 - 2,999,999
- ◉ 100,000 - 499,999

SCALE 1:21,000,000   OPTIMAL CONFORMAL PROJECTION

MILES
0   300   600   900
KILOMETERS
0   300   600   900

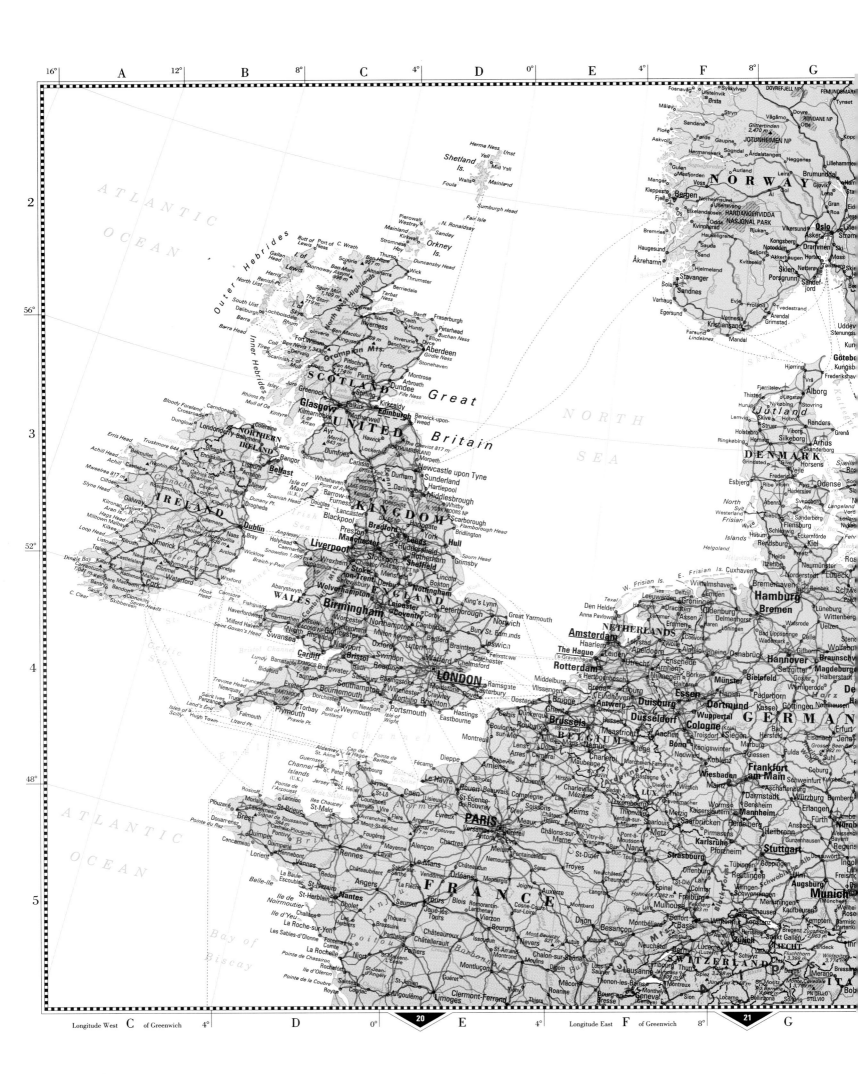

Western and Central Europe

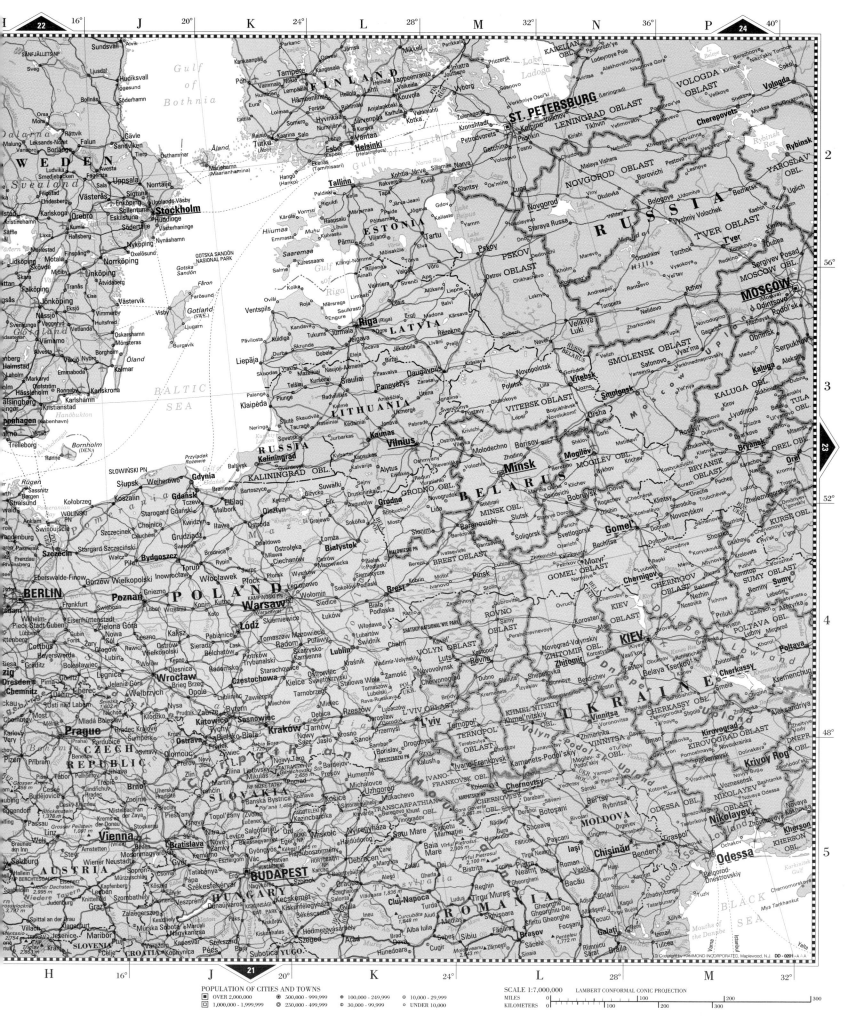

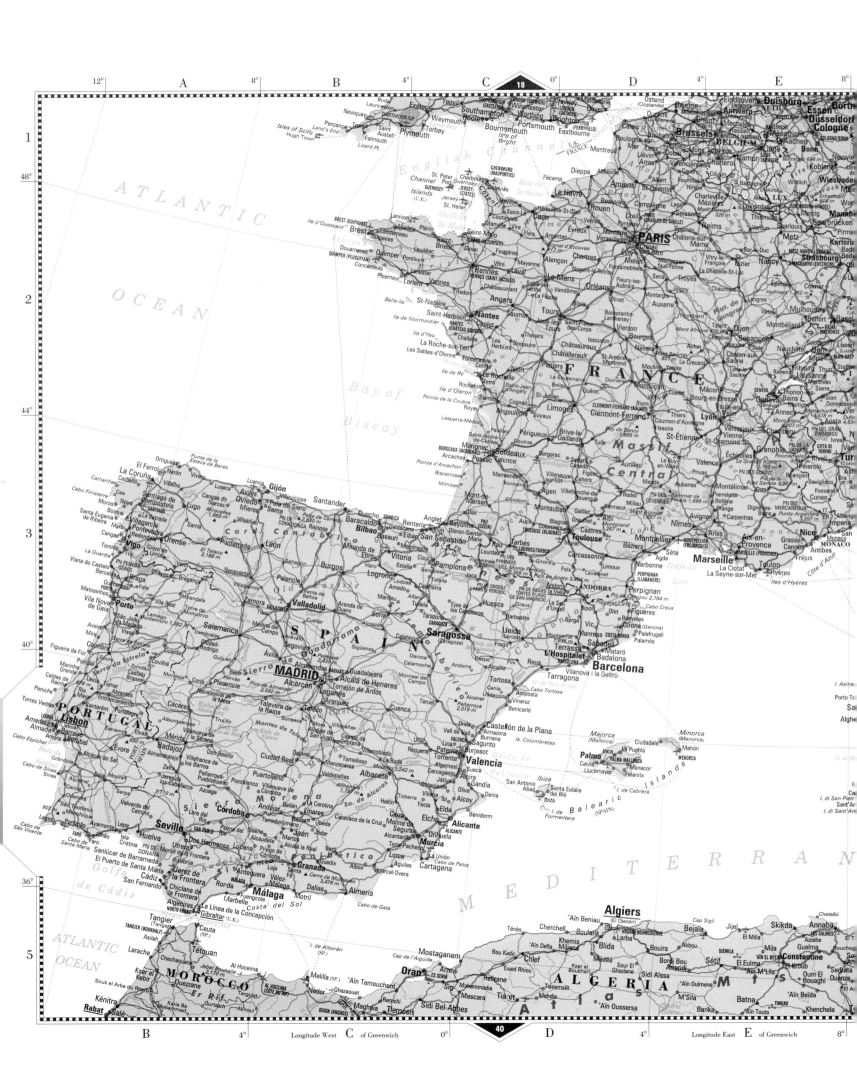

Southern Europe

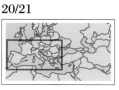

POPULATION OF CITIES AND TOWNS

■ OVER 2,000,000	● 500,000 - 999,999	● 100,000 - 249,999
◻ 1,000,000 - 1,999,999	● 250,000 - 499,999	● 30,000 - 99,999
		● 10,000 - 29,999
		○ UNDER 10,000

SCALE 1:7,000,000   LAMBERT CONFORMAL CONIC PROJECTION

MILES 0   100   200   300

KILOMETERS 0   100   200   300

© Copyright by HAMMOND INCORPORATED, Maplewood, N.J. DD - 0202 - A - A

Scandinavia and Finland, Iceland

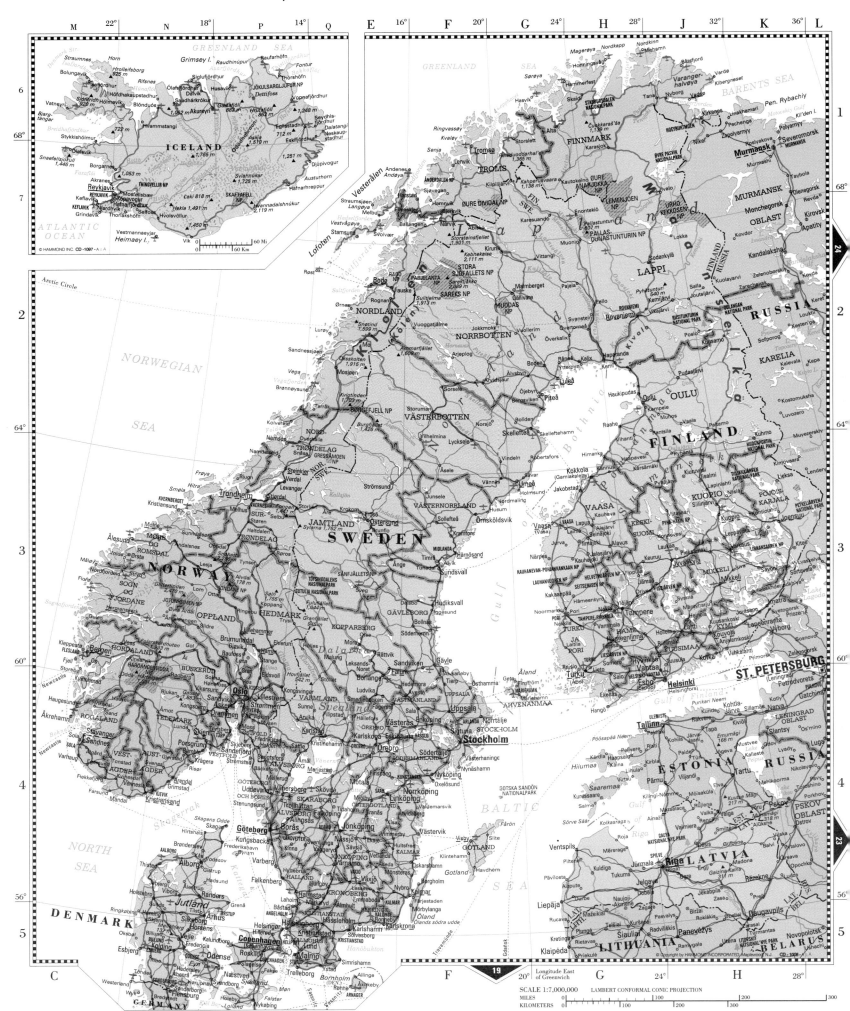

Eastern Europe and Turkey

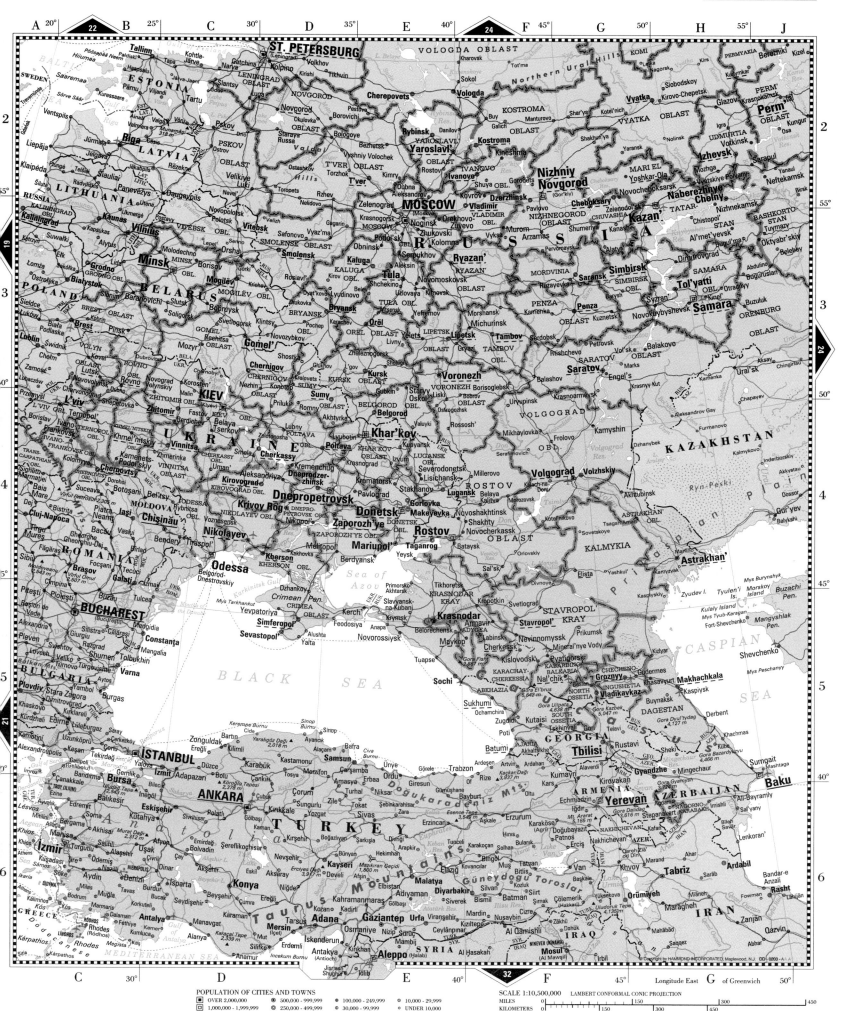

POPULATION OF CITIES AND TOWNS

■ OVER 2,000,000	● 500,000 - 999,999
▣ 1,000,000 - 1,999,999	● 250,000 - 499,999
	● 100,000 - 249,999
	● 30,000 - 99,999
○ 10,000 - 29,999	
○ UNDER 10,000	

SCALE 1:10,500,000   LAMBERT CONFORMAL CONIC PROJECTION

MILES   0   150   300   450

KILOMETERS   0   150   300   450

Longitude East of Greenwich

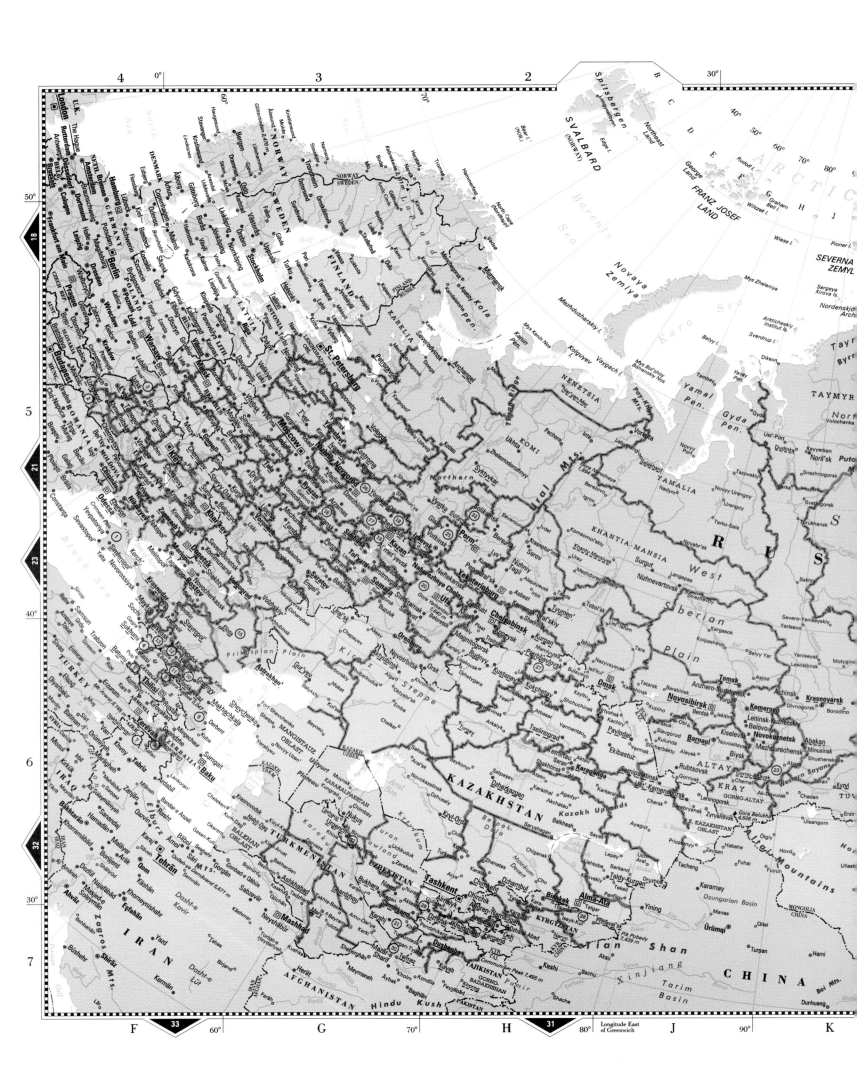

Russia and Neighboring Countries

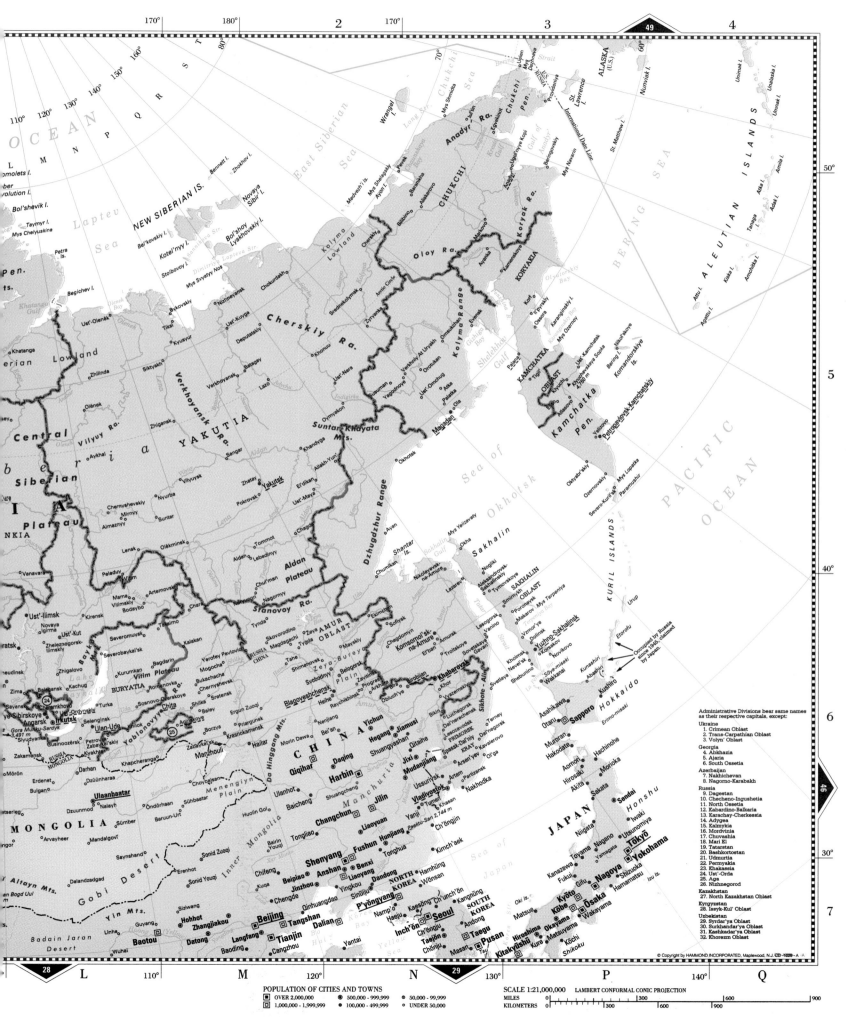

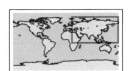

Asia - Physical

AREA OF OPTIMIZATION

The red band which surrounds these physical and political maps defines the "Area of Optimization." Within this bounding curve is the most accurate conformal map that can be made of the region. Outside the optimized area, distortion increases rapidly, and tears or other irregularities in the grid may occur. (See page 3 for additional information.)

SCALE 1:49,000,000 OPTIMAL CONFORMAL PROJECTION

MILES 0 · 700 · 1400 · 2100

KILOMETERS 0 · 700 · 1400 · 2100

POPULATION OF CITIES AND TOWNS

☐ OVER 3,000,000   ● 500,000 - 999,999   ○ UNDER 100,000

☐ 1,000,000 - 2,999,999   ● 100,000 - 499,999

Longitude East F of Greenwich

© Copyright by HAMMOND INCORPORATED, Maplewood, N.J. CD · 1090 · A · A

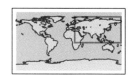

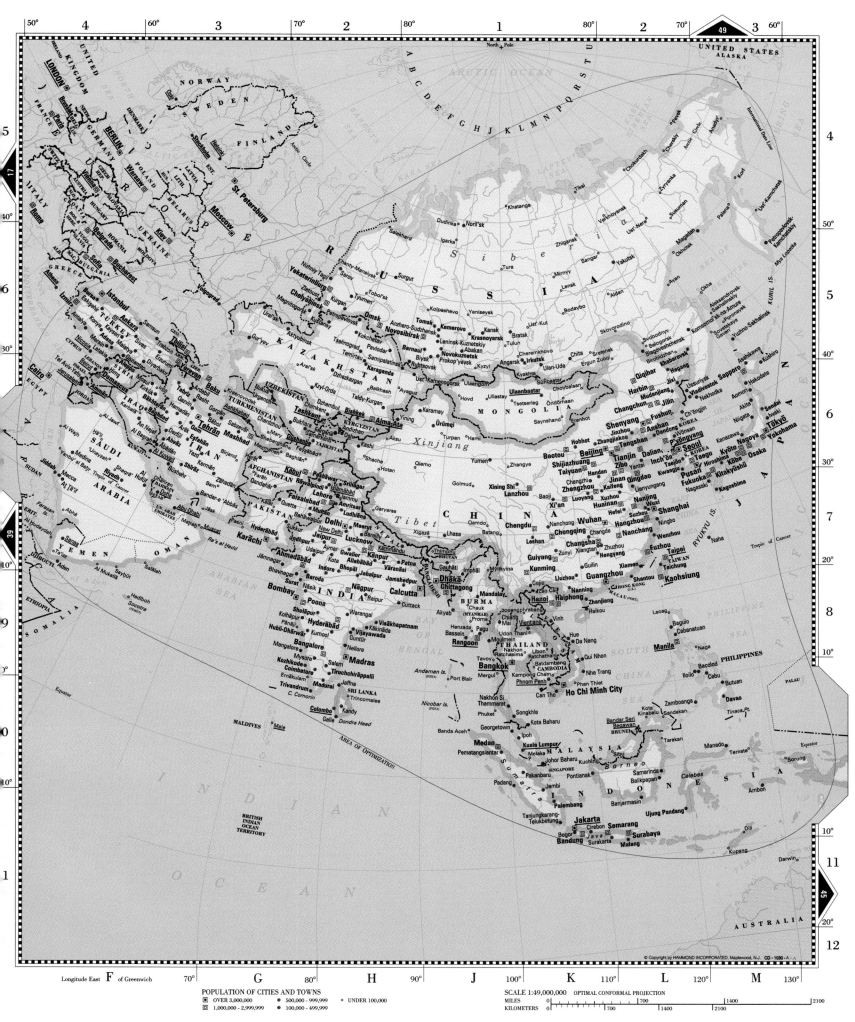

POPULATION OF CITIES AND TOWNS

◻ OVER 3,000,000　● 500,000 - 999,999　○ UNDER 100,000

◻ 1,000,000 - 2,999,999　● 100,000 - 499,999

SCALE 1:49,000,000　OPTIMAL CONFORMAL PROJECTION

MILES　0　700　1400　2100

KILOMETERS　0　700　1400　2100

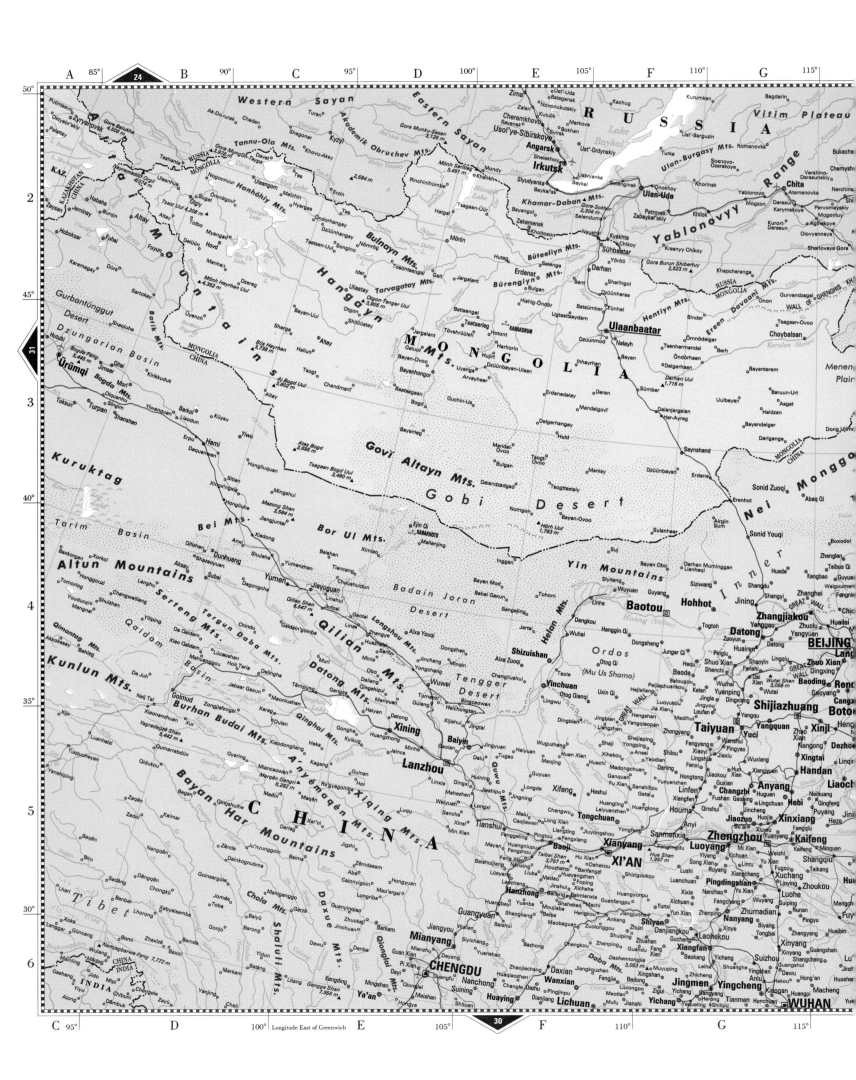

Eastern Asia

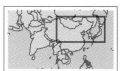

POPULATION OF CITIES AND TOWNS

| ■ OVER 2,000,000 | ⊞ 500,000 - 999,999 | ● 100,000 - 249,999 | • 10,000 - 29,999 |
| ⊡ 1,000,000 - 1,999,999 | ⊕ 250,000 - 499,999 | ⊙ 30,000 - 99,999 | ∘ UNDER 10,000 |

SCALE 1:10,500,000   LAMBERT CONFORMAL CONIC PROJECTION

MILES 0   150   150   300   450

KILOMETERS 0   150   300   450

Southeastern China, Taiwan, Philippines

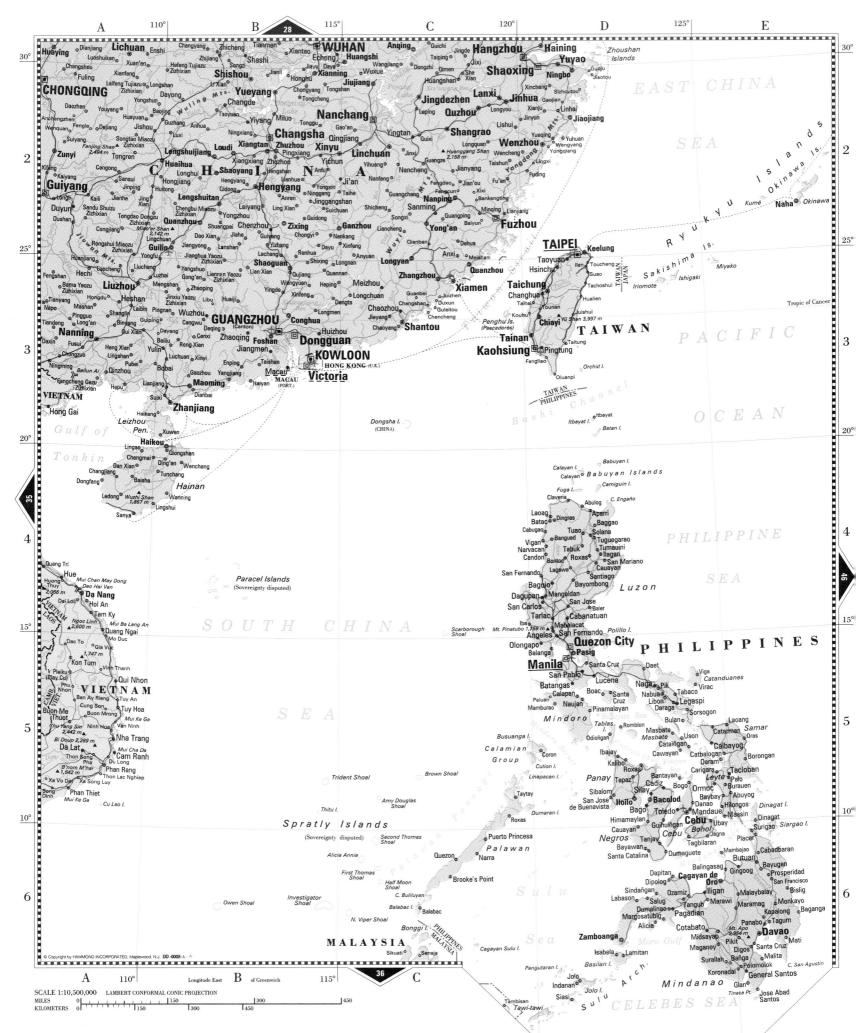

Central Asia

POPULATION OF CITIES AND TOWNS

■ OVER 2,000,000   ● 500,000 - 999,999   ● 100,000 - 249,999   ● 10,000 - 29,999
□ 1,000,000 - 1,999,999   ● 250,000 - 499,999   ● 30,000 - 99,999   ○ UNDER 10,000

SCALE 1:10,500,000   LAMBERT CONFORMAL CONIC PROJECTION

MILES 0   150   300   450

KILOMETERS 0   150   300   450

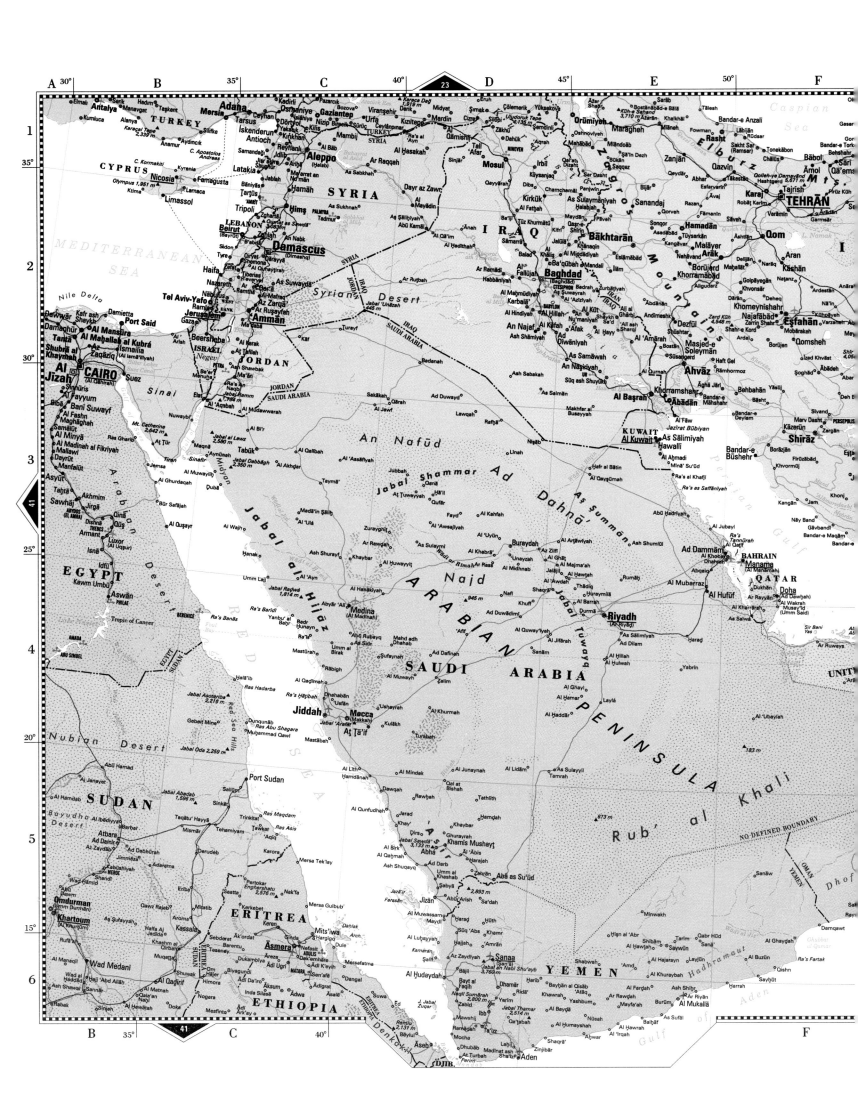

Southwestern Asia

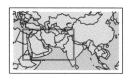

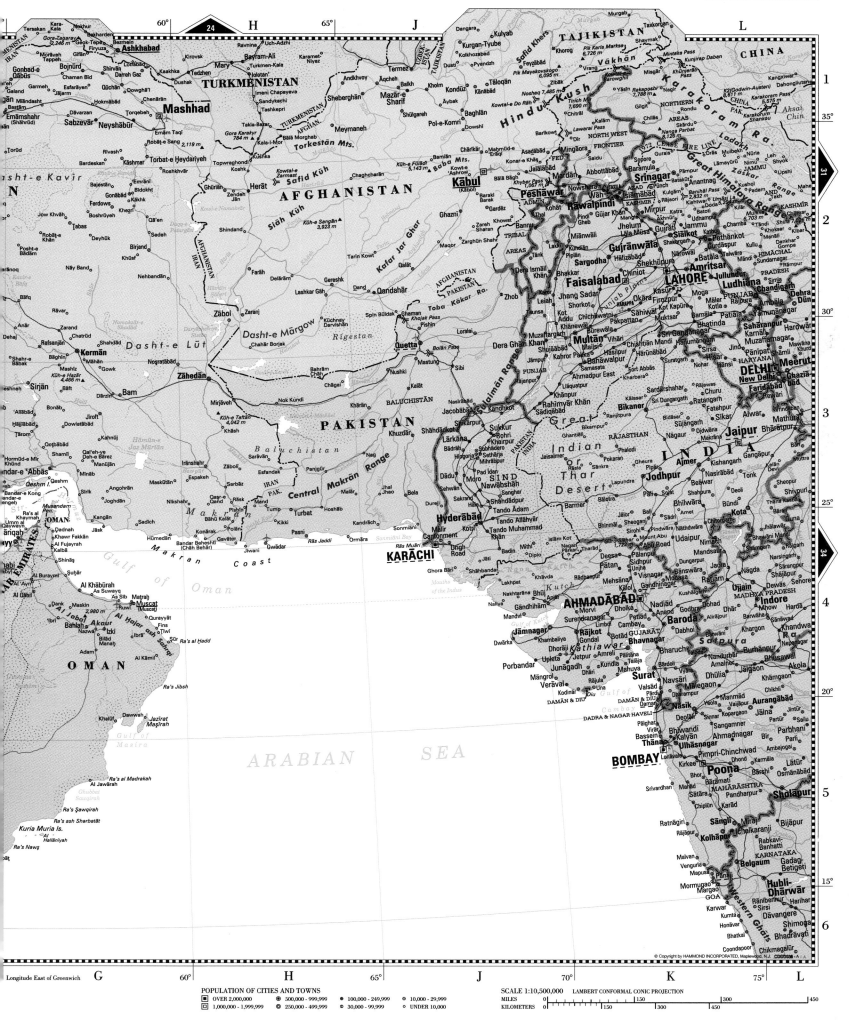

Longitude East of Greenwich

POPULATION OF CITIES AND TOWNS

- ▣ OVER 2,000,000
- ▣ 1,000,000 – 1,999,999
- ■ 500,000 – 999,999
- ■ 250,000 – 499,999
- ● 100,000 – 249,999
- ● 30,000 – 99,999
- ● 10,000 – 29,999
- ○ UNDER 10,000

SCALE 1:10,500,000 LAMBERT CONFORMAL CONIC PROJECTION

MILES 0 · 150 · 300 · 450

KILOMETERS 0 · 150 · 300 · 450

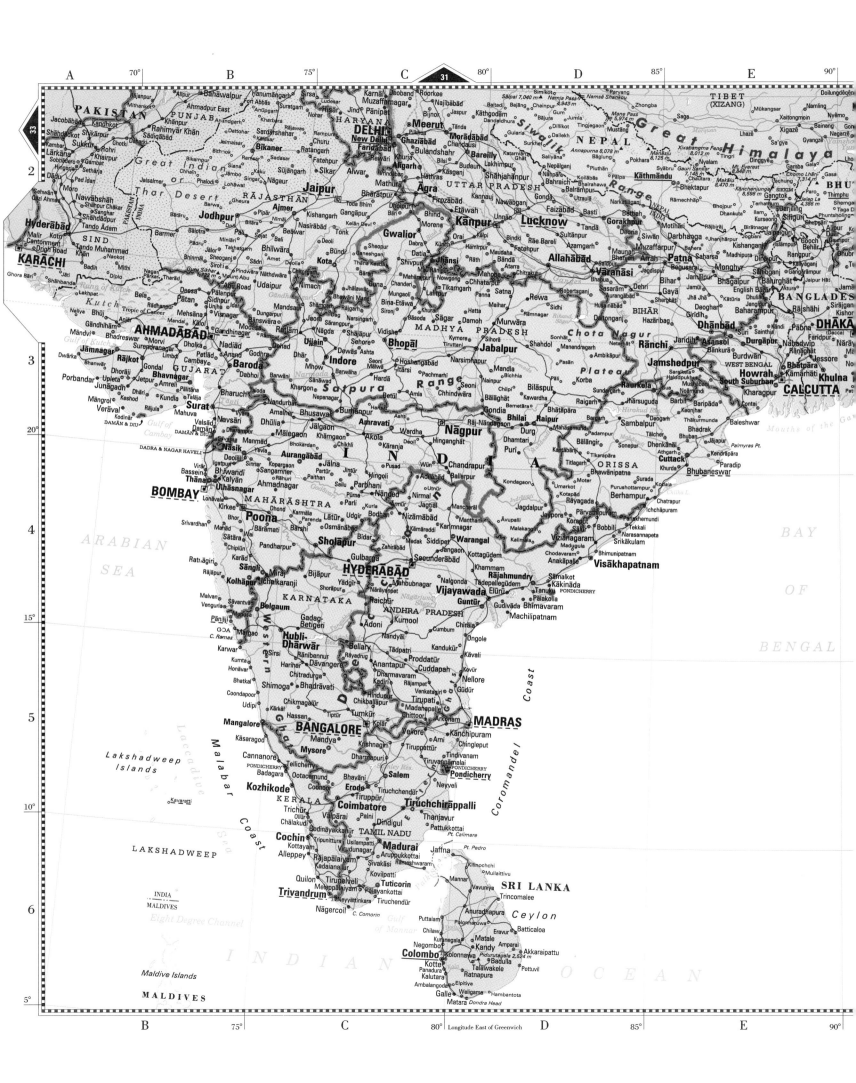

Southern Asia

POPULATION OF CITIES AND TOWNS

■ OVER 2,000,000	◉ 500,000 - 999,999	⊕ 100,000 - 249,999	○ 10,000 - 29,999
▣ 1,000,000 - 1,999,999	◉ 250,000 - 499,999	⊕ 30,000 - 99,999	○ UNDER 10,000

SCALE 1:10,500,000   LAMBERT CONFORMAL CONIC PROJECTION

MILES 0 — 150 — 300 — 450
KILOMETERS 0 — 150 — 300 — 450

© Copyright by HAMMOND INCORPORATED, Maplewood, N.J. **CD - 1041 - A - A**

SCALE 1:10,500,000   LAMBERT CONFORMAL CONIC PROJECTION

MILES   0   150   300   450
KILOMETERS 0   150   300   450

POPULATION OF CITIES AND TOWNS

■ OVER 2,000,000 ● 500,000 - 999,999 ● 100,000 - 249,999 ○ 10,000 - 29,999
□ 1,000,000 - 1,999,999 ◉ 250,000 - 499,999 ● 30,000 - 99,999 ∘ UNDER 10,000

Longitude East of Greenwich

Southeastern Asia

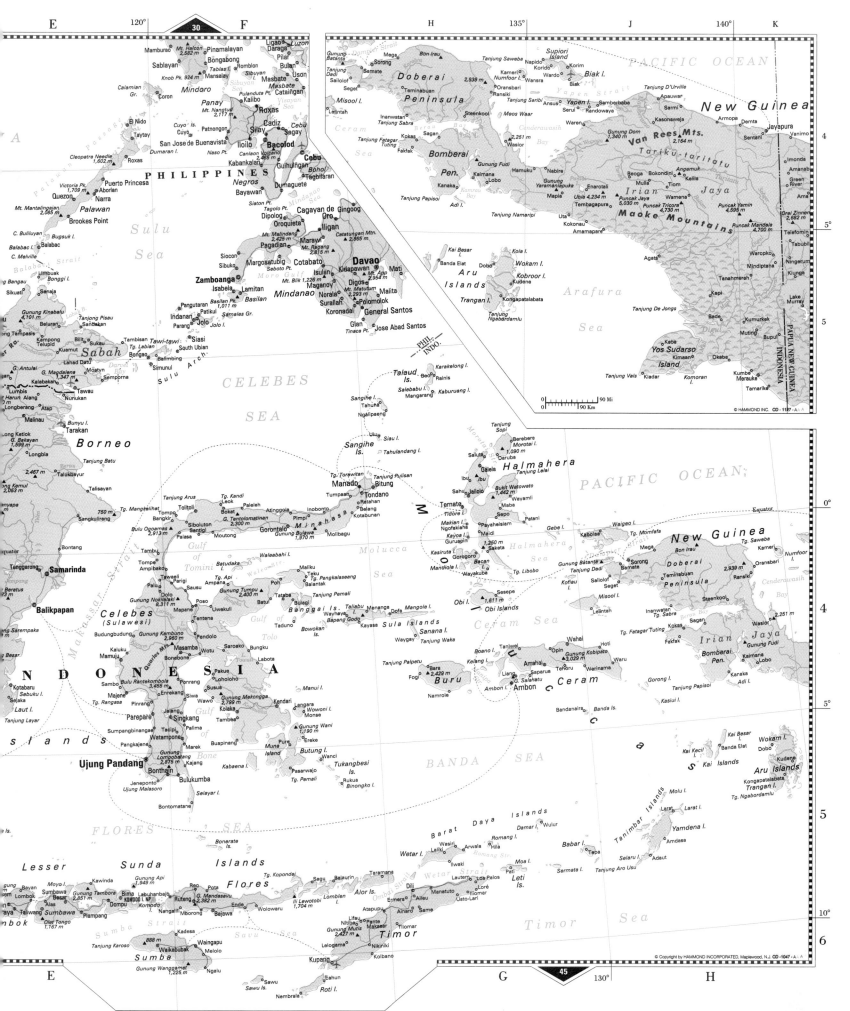

Africa - Physical

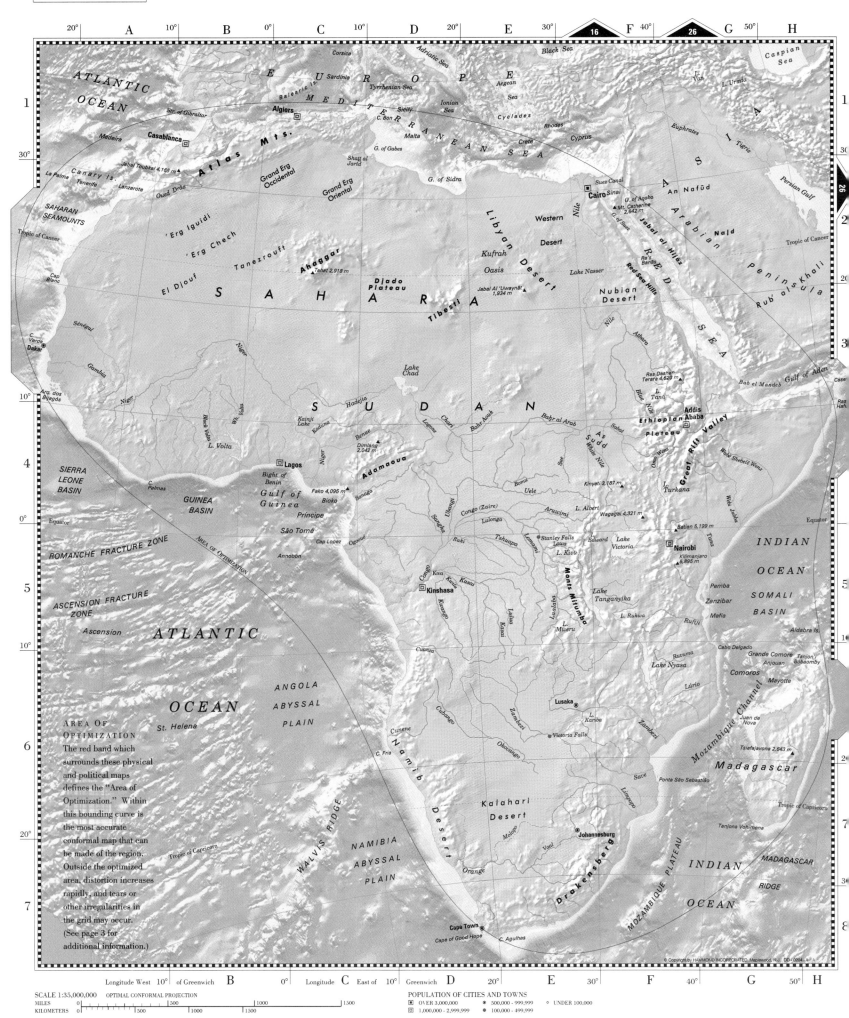

AREA OF
OPTIMIZATION
The red band which
surrounds these physical
and political maps
defines the "Area of
Optimization." Within
this bounding curve is
the most accurate
conformal map that can
be made of the region.
Outside the optimized
area, distortion increases
rapidly, and tears or
other irregularities in
the grid may occur.
(See page 3 for
additional information.)

SCALE 1:35,000,000   OPTIMAL CONFORMAL PROJECTION

MILES   0   500   1000   1500
KILOMETERS 0   500   1000   1500

POPULATION OF CITIES AND TOWNS
■ OVER 3,000,000   ● 500,000 - 999,999   ○ UNDER 100,000
▣ 1,000,000 - 2,999,999   ◆ 100,000 - 499,999

© Copyright by HAMMOND INCORPORATED, Maplewood, N.J. DD-0064-A A

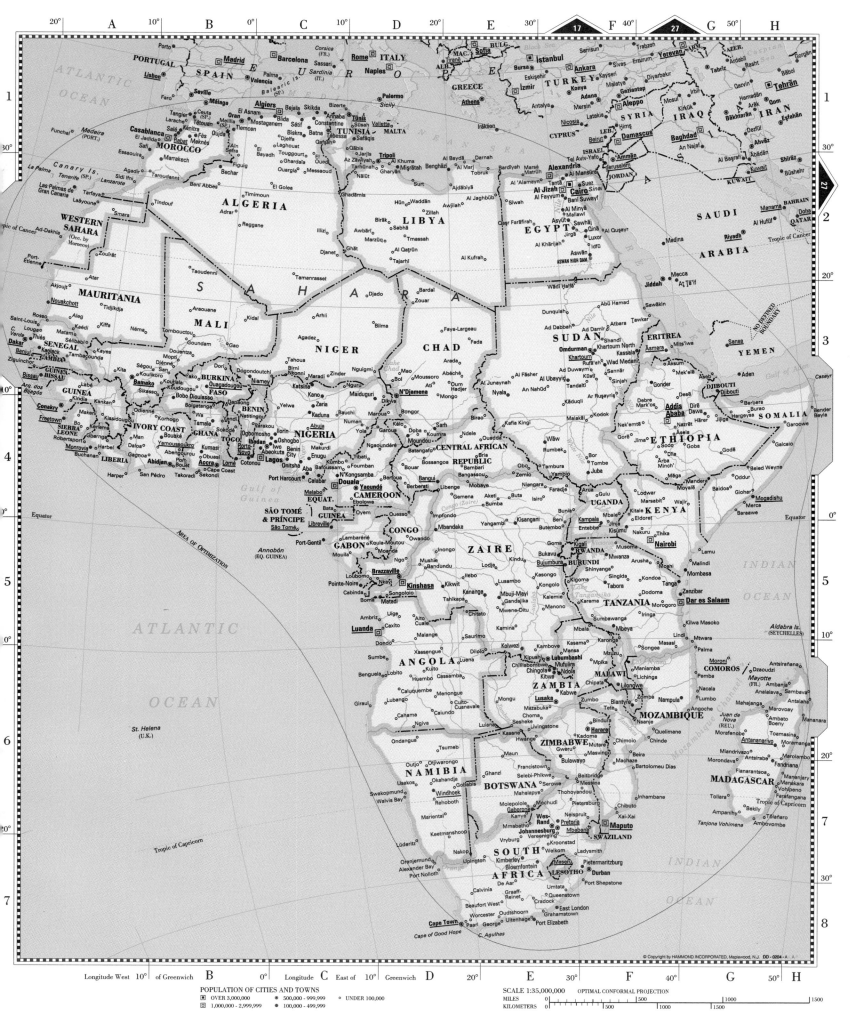

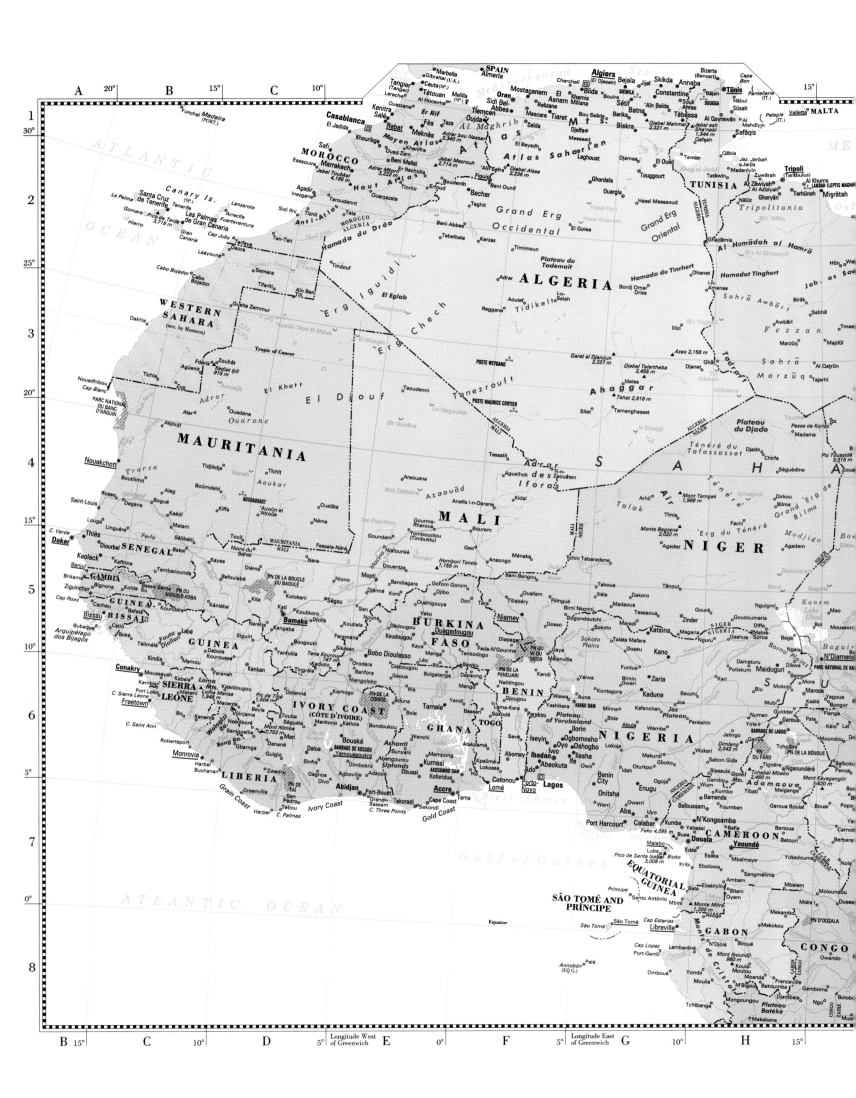

Northern Africa

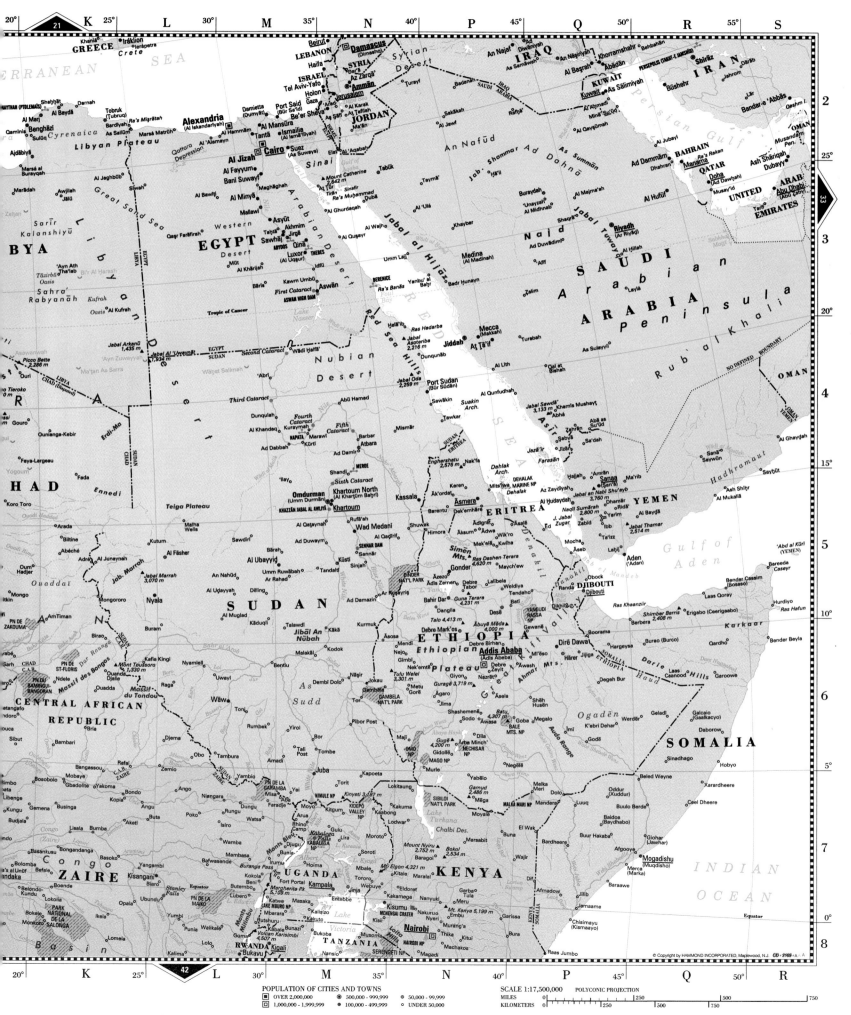

POPULATION OF CITIES AND TOWNS

- ◼ OVER 2,000,000
- ◼ 1,000,000 - 1,999,999
- ● 500,000 - 999,999
- ● 100,000 - 499,999
- ● 50,000 - 99,999
- ○ UNDER 50,000

SCALE 1:17,500,000   POLYCONIC PROJECTION

MILES 0   250   500   750

KILOMETERS 0   250   500   750

Southern Africa

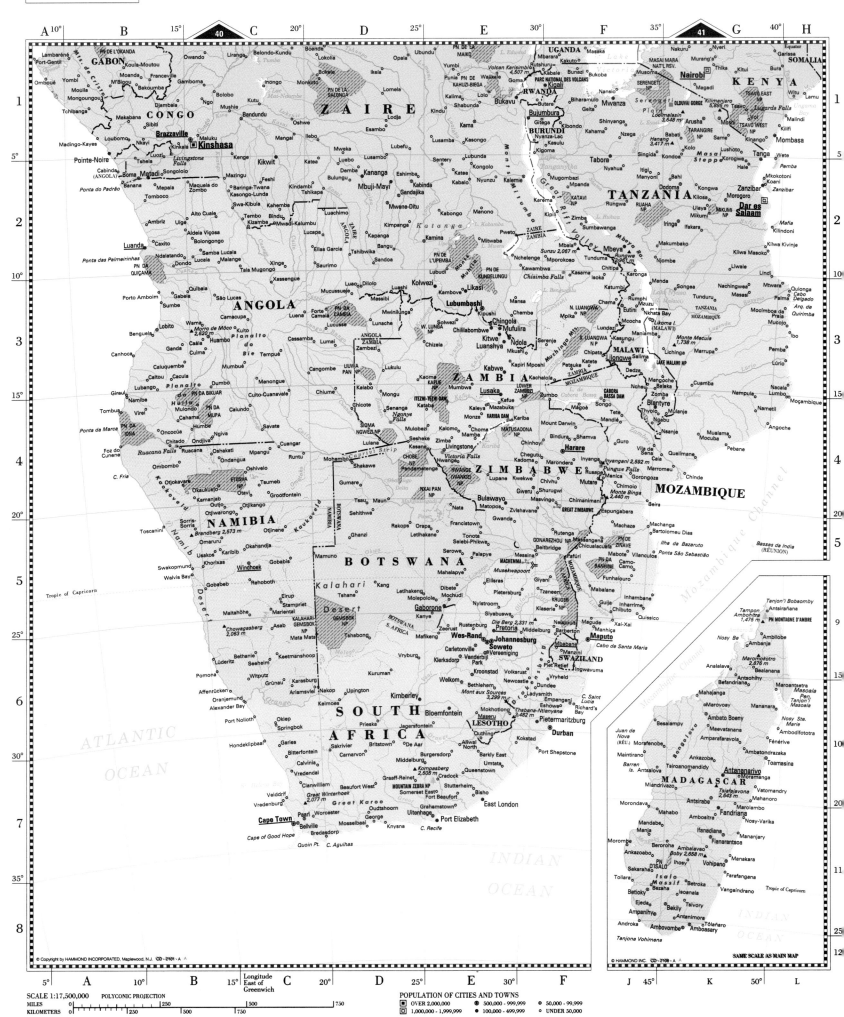

SAME SCALE AS MAIN MAP

SCALE 1:17,500,000   POLYCONIC PROJECTION

MILES

KILOMETERS

POPULATION OF CITIES AND TOWNS

▣ OVER 2,000,000	● 500,000 - 999,999	○ 50,000 - 99,999
▣ 1,000,000 - 1,999,999	● 100,000 - 499,999	○ UNDER 50,000

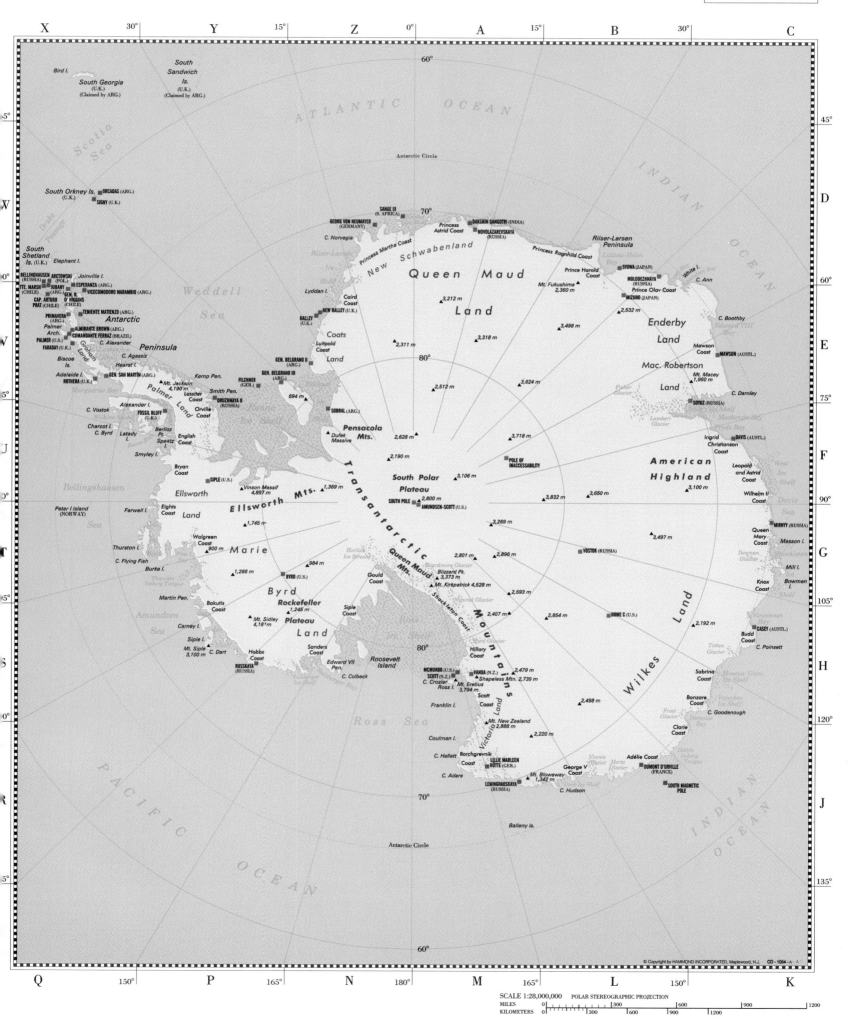

Australia, New Zealand - Physical

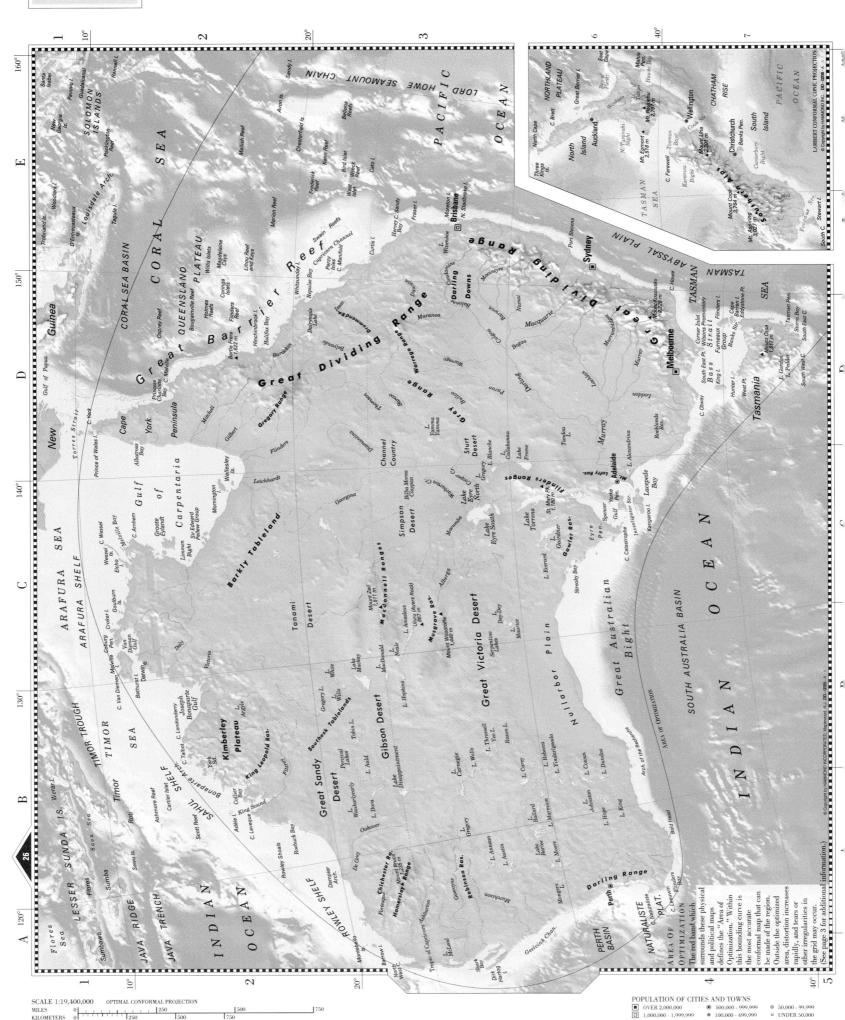

SCALE 1:19,400,000   OPTIMAL CONFORMAL PROJECTION

MILES 0 | 250 | 500 | 750

KILOMETERS 0 | 250 | 500 | 750

POPULATION OF CITIES AND TOWNS
■ OVER 2,000,000 ◉ 500,000 - 999,999 ⊛ 50,000 - 99,999
▣ 1,000,000 - 1,999,999 ◉ 100,000 - 499,999 ○ UNDER 50,000

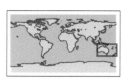

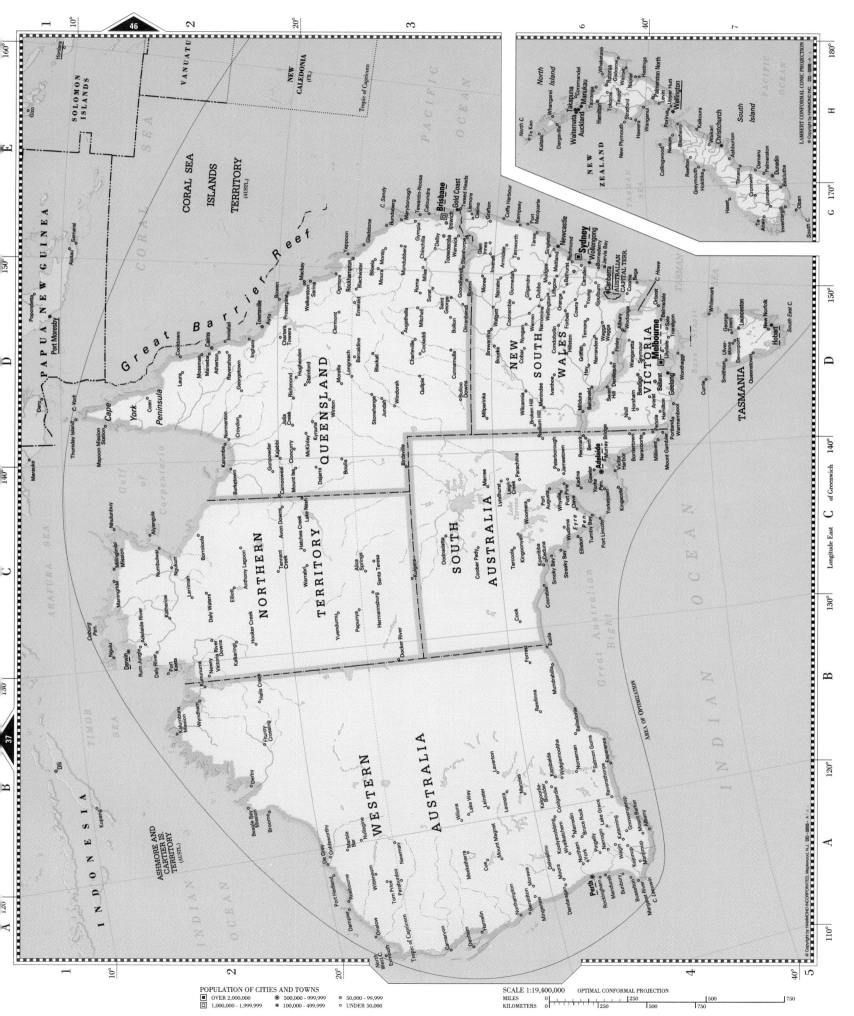

POPULATION OF CITIES AND TOWNS

- ▣ OVER 2,000,000
- ▣ 1,000,000 - 1,999,999
- ⊚ 500,000 - 999,999
- ⊙ 100,000 - 499,999
- ⊙ 50,000 - 99,999
- ○ UNDER 50,000

SCALE 1:19,400,000   OPTIMAL CONFORMAL PROJECTION

MILES   0   250   500   750
KILOMETERS   0   250   500   750

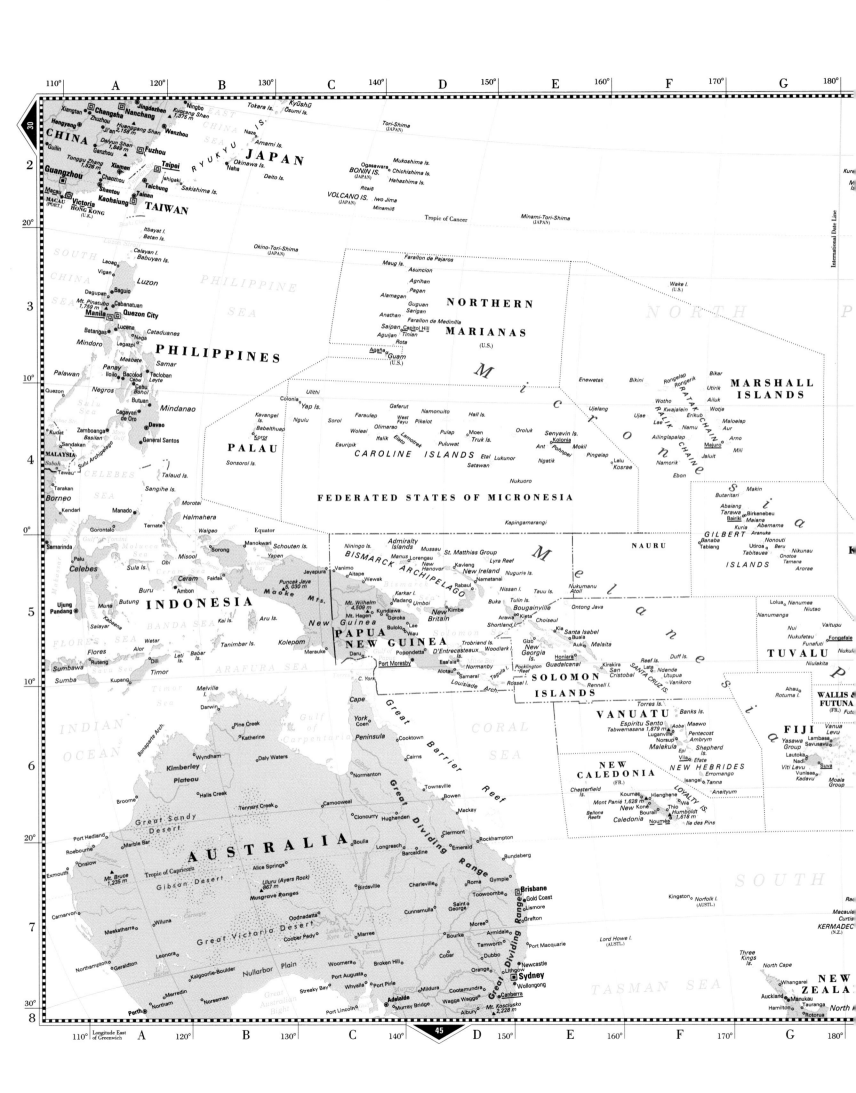

A 110° B 120° C 130° D 140° E 150° F 160° G 170° 180°

2 30°

CHINA

Xiangtan Changsha Nanchang Jingdezhen Ningbo
Hengyang Zhuzhou Kuoçang Shan ▲ 1,375 m
Huanggang Shan Wenzhou
Guilin Tonggu Zhang Daiyun Shan Ji'an 2,158 m
1,526 m Ganzhou 1,849 m Fuzhou
Guangzhou Xiamen Taipei
Macau Chaozhou Taichung
MACAU Victoria Shantou Tainan
(PORT.) Kaohsiung
HONG KONG **TAIWAN**
(U.K.)

Tokara Is.
Kyūshū
Ōsumi Is.

JAPAN

Naze Amami Is.
Okinawa Is.
Naha
Ishigaki Sakishima Is.
Daito Is.

Tori-Shima (JAPAN)

Mukoshima Is.
Ogasawara Chichishima Is.
BONIN IS. Hahashima Is.
(JAPAN)
Ritaiô
VOLCANO IS. Iwo Jima
(JAPAN)
Minamiiô

Minami-Tori-Shima (JAPAN)

Tropic of Cancer

20°

SOUTH CHINA SEA

Itbayat I.
Batan Is.
Calayan I.
Babuyan Is.

PHILIPPINE SEA

Farallon de Pajaros

Maug Is. Asuncion

Agrihan

Pagan

Alamagan

Anathan Guguan
Sarigan

Saipan Farallon de Medinilla
Capitol Hill
Aguijan Tinian
Rota

Agaña Guam
(U.S.)

NORTHERN

MARIANAS

(U.S.)

Wake I.
(U.S.)

NORTH

3 30°

Laoag

Vigan **Luzon**
Baguio
Dagupan Cabanatuan
Mt. Pinatubo
1,759 m Quezon City
Manila Lucena
Batangas Naga Catanduanes
Mindoro Legazpi

Masbate Samar
Panay Iloilo Tacloban
Bacolod Cebu Leyte
Negros Bohol
Butuan
Cagayan
Palawan de Oro
Quezon **Mindanao**
Zamboanga Davao
Kudat Basilan
Sandakan General Santos
MALAYSIA
Sabah
Tawau Sulu Archipelago

PHILIPPINES

Ulithi
Colonia Yap Is.
Kayangel
Is. Ngulu Sorol
Babelthuap
Koror
PALAU
Sonsorol Is.

Gaferut
Faraulep West
Fayu Namonuito
Woleai Olimarao Pikelot
Ifalik Pulap Hall Is.
Eauripik Lamotrek Moen
Satawal Elato Puluwat Truk Is.
Woleai
Oroluk
Senyavin Is.
Ant Kolonia
Lukunor Pohnpei Mokil
Ngatik Pingelap

CAROLINE ISLANDS Etal
Satawan

Nukuoro

Enewetak Bikini
Rongelap Bikar
Rongerik
Ujelang Wotho Utirik
Ujae Kwajalein Erikub Ailuk
Lae Namu Wotje
Ailinglapalap Maloelap
Aur
Namorik Arno
Lelu Jaluit Majuro
Kosrae Ebon Mili

MARSHALL
ISLANDS

RATAK CHAIN
RALIK CHAIN

FEDERATED STATES OF MICRONESIA

Kapingamarangi

Makin
Butaritari
Abaiang
Tarawa Birkenebeu
Bairiki Maiana
Kuria Abemama

GILBERT

Banaba Nonouti
Beru Nikunau
Tabiang Onotoa Tamana
Tabiteuea Arorae

ISLANDS

M i c r o n e s i a

4 30°

CELEBES SEA

Tarakan
Borneo
Kendari
Samarinda

Manado
Gorontalo

Ternate
Morotai

Talaud Is.
Sangihe Is.
Halmahera

Waigeo Schouten Is.
Misool Manokwari Yapen
Sorong

Obi
Sula Is.
Ceram Fakfak
Buru Ambon

Equator

0°

Samarinda

INDONESIA
Celebes
Ujung
Pandang
Muna Butung
Salayar
Kabaena

Palu

BANDA SEA

Wetar
Flores Alor
Sumbawa Ruteng
Sumba Timor
Kupang

Kai Is.
Aru Is.
Tanimbar Is.

Babar
Leti Is.

FLORES SEA

Maoke Mts.
Puncak Jaya
5,030 m
Jayapura Vanimo
Aitape Wewak
New Guinea
Mt. Wilhelm
4,509 m Madang
Mt. Hagen Goroka
Kundiawa Lae
Bulolo
Kolepom
Merauke
Daru
Port Moresby
PAPUA
NEW GUINEA

Niningo Is. Admiralty
Islands Mussau
Lorengau St. Matthias Group
Manus New
Hanover
Kavieng New Ireland
Namatanai
Rabaul
Bismarck
New
Britain Kimbe
Nissan I.
Tauu Is.
Buka
Bougainville
Arawa Kieta
Shortland I.

Lyra Reef
Nuguris Is.

Nukumanu
Atoll

Ontong Java

BISMARCK ARCHIPELAGO

Trobriand Is.
D'Entrecasteaux
Is. Woodlark I.
Normanby
Esa'ala
Alotau Samarai
Louisiade Arch.

NAURU

M e l a n e s i a

5 30°

Gizo
New
Georgia
Is.
Honiara
Guadalcanal

Kia Santa Isabel
Buala
Auki Malaita

Kirakira
San
Cristobal
Rennell I.

Reef Is. Duff Is.
Santa
Cruz Is.
Ndende
Lata Utupua
Vanikoro

Lolua Nanumea
Nanumanga Niutao
Vaitupu
Nui
Nukufetau Funafuti
Fongafale
Niulakita

TUVALU

P o l y n e s i a

10°

C. York
Cape
York
Peninsula

Torres Str.

VANUATU
Espiritu Santo
Tabwemasana 1,879 m
Luganville Maewo
Norsup Pentecost
Malekula Ambrym
Epi Shepherd
Vila Is.
Efate

NEW HEBRIDES
Erromango
Isangel Tanna
Aneityum

Banks Is.

Ahau
Rotuma I.

Lolua Nanumea

WALLIS &
FUTUNA
(FR.)

FIJI
Yasawa Vanua
Group Levu
Lambasa
Savusavu
Lautoka
Nadi Suva
Viti Levu
Vunisea
Kadavu Moala
Group

6 30°

Kimberley
Plateau
Halls Creek

Darwin
Pine Creek
Katherine

Melville
I.

Gulf of Carpentaria

Cooktown
Cairns

CORAL SEA

NEW
CALEDONIA
(FR.)

Chesterfield
Is.
Mont Panié 1,628 m
New Koné
Bourail
Bella Caledonia Noumea
Reefs

Koumac
Hienghene
Thio Wé
Humboldt
1,618 m
Ile des Pins

LOYALTY IS.

M i c r o n e s i a

Broome

Wyndham
Daly Waters

Normanton
Townsville

Bowen
Mackay

Rockhampton

Kingston Norfolk I.
(AUSTL.)

SOUTH

7 30°

Port Hedland
Roebourne Marble Bar
Onslow
Mt. Bruce
1,235 m

Great Sandy Desert

Tennant Creek
Camooweal
Cloncurry Hughenden
Boulia

Longreach
Barcaldine
Clermont
Emerald
Bundaberg

Exmouth
Carnarvon

AUSTRALIA

Alice Springs
Tropic of Capricorn
Uluru (Ayers Rock)
867 m
Musgrave Ranges

Gibson Desert

Birdsville
Charleville
Roma
Toowoomba
Gympie
Brisbane
Gold Coast
Lismore

Great Dividing Range

Lord Howe I.
(AUSTL.)

Three
Kings
Is.

KERMADEC
(N.Z.)

TASMAN SEA

North Cape
Whangarei
Auckland Manukau
Hamilton Tauranga
Rotorua

NEW
ZEALA

8 30°

Geraldton
Northampton
Meekatharra
Wiluna Leonora

Kalgoorlie-Boulder
Nullarbor Plain
Norseman

Oodnadatta
Coober Pedy
Marree
Woomera
Port Augusta
Whyalla
Port Pirie
Port Lincoln
Adelaide
Murray Bridge

Great Victoria Desert

Streaky Bay

Northam
Perth

Broken Hill
Cobar
Dubbo
Orange
Bathurst
Lithgow **Sydney**
Wollongong
Mt. Kosciusko
2,228 m
Canberra
Albury

Bourke
Tamworth
Armidale
Port Macquarie

Moree
Saint
George
Grafton

Cunnamulla
Cootamundra
Wagga Wagga
Mildura

North I

110° Longitude East A 120° B 130° C 140° D 150° E 160° F 170° G 180°
of Greenwich

Central Pacific Ocean

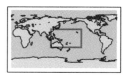

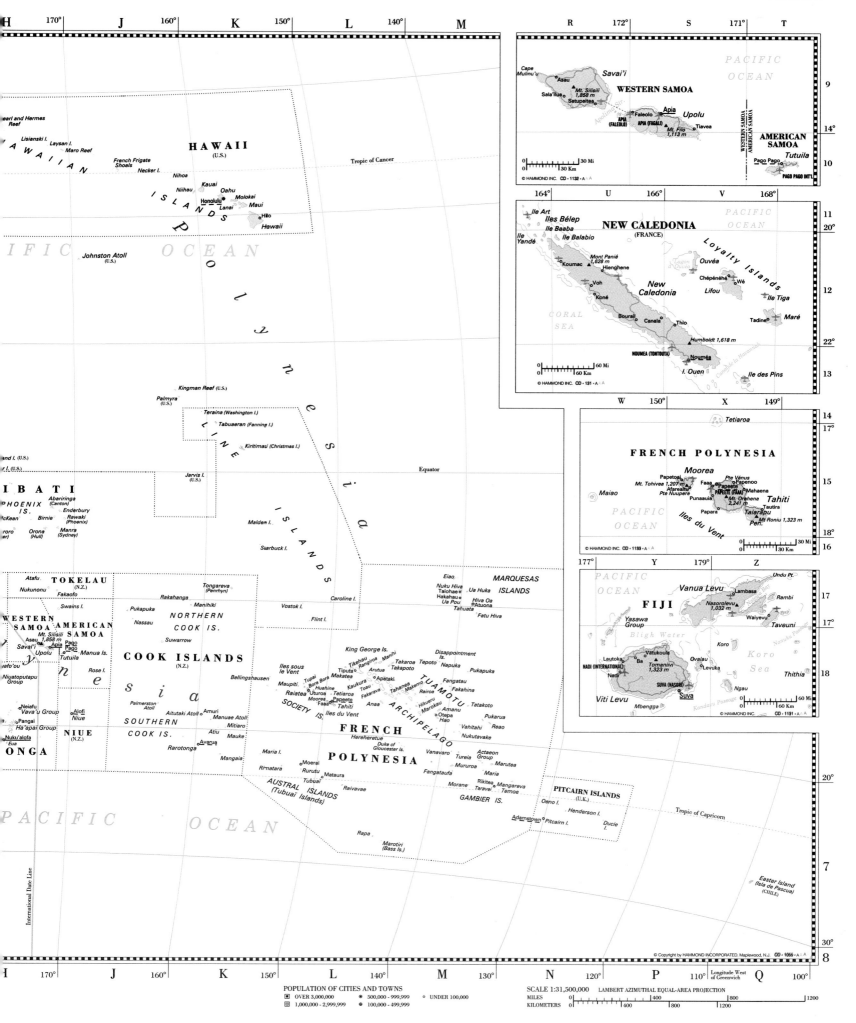

North America - Physical

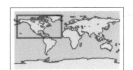

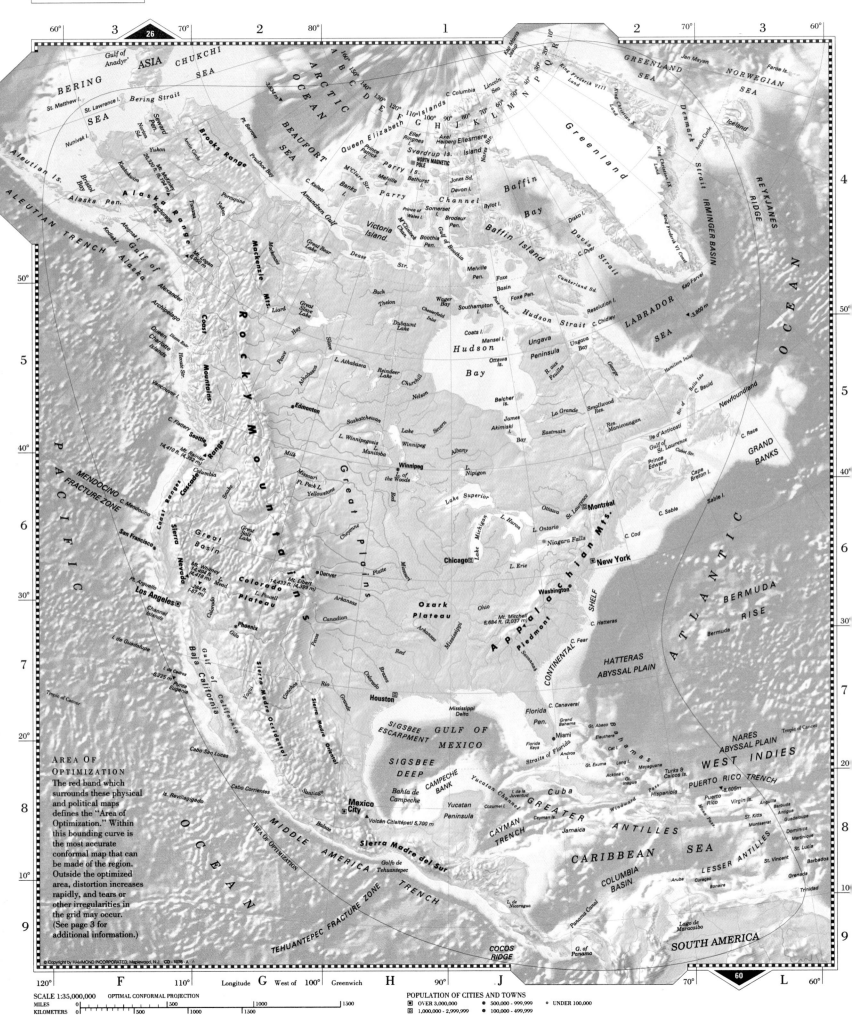

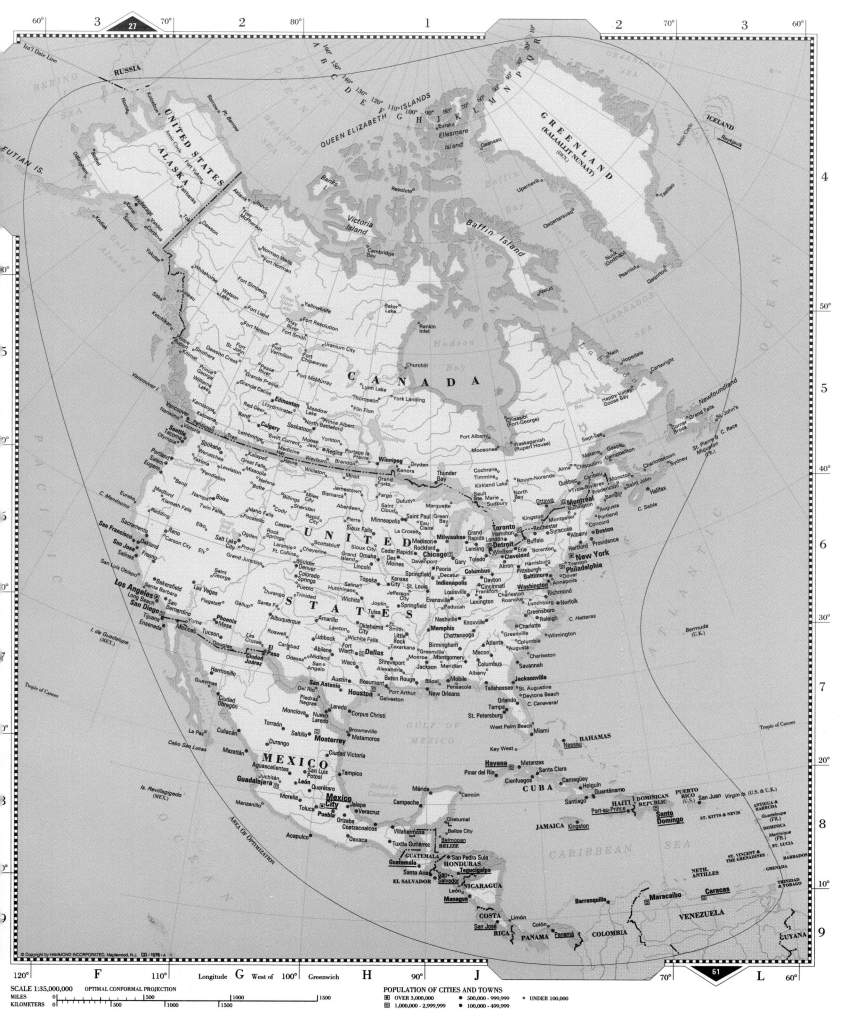

SCALE 1:35,000,000   OPTIMAL CONFORMAL PROJECTION

MILES 0   500   1000   1500

KILOMETERS 0   500   1000   1500

POPULATION OF CITIES AND TOWNS

■ OVER 3,000,000   ● 500,000 - 999,999   ○ UNDER 100,000

◻ 1,000,000 - 2,999,999   ● 100,000 - 499,999

Southwestern Canada, Northwestern United States

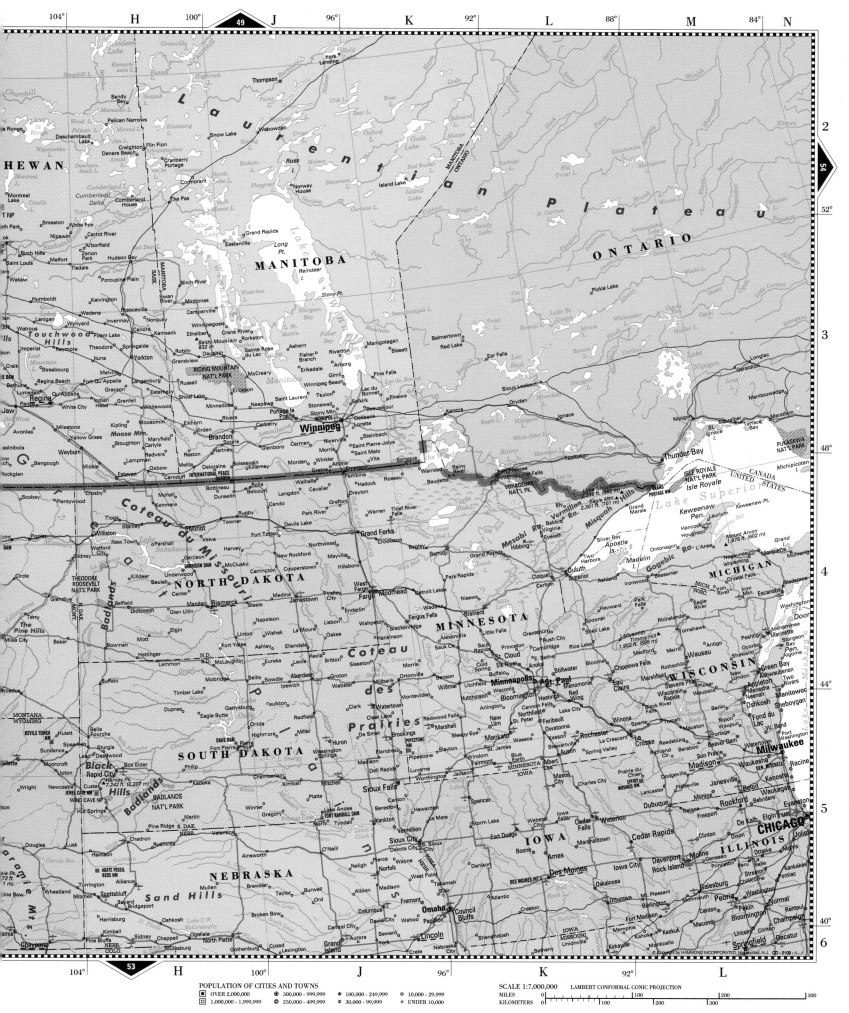

Southwestern United States

POPULATION OF CITIES AND TOWNS

- OVER 2,000,000
- 1,000,000 - 1,999,999
- 500,000 - 999,999
- 250,000 - 499,999
- 100,000 - 249,999
- 30,000 - 99,999
- 10,000 - 29,999
- UNDER 10,000

SCALE 1:7,000,000   LAMBERT CONFORMAL CONIC PROJECTION

MILES 0   100   200   300
KILOMETERS 0   100   200   300

© Copyright by HAMMOND INCORPORATED, Maplewood, N.J.   CD-2110-A-A

Southeastern Canada, Northeastern United States

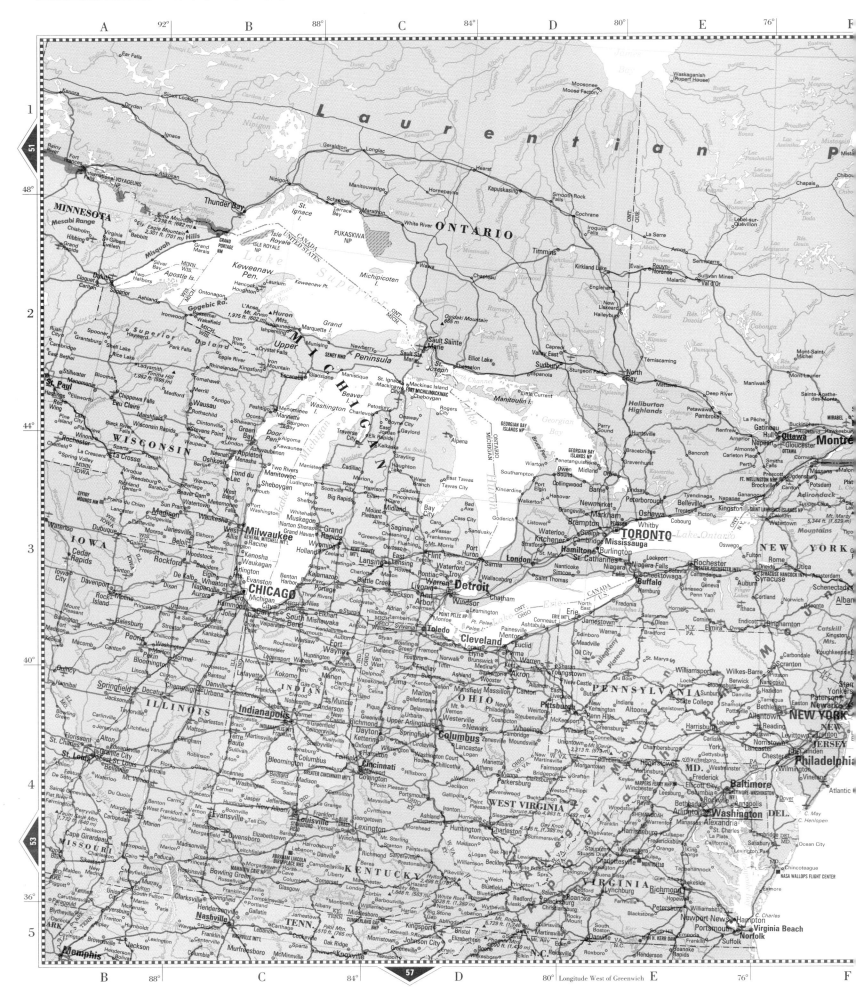

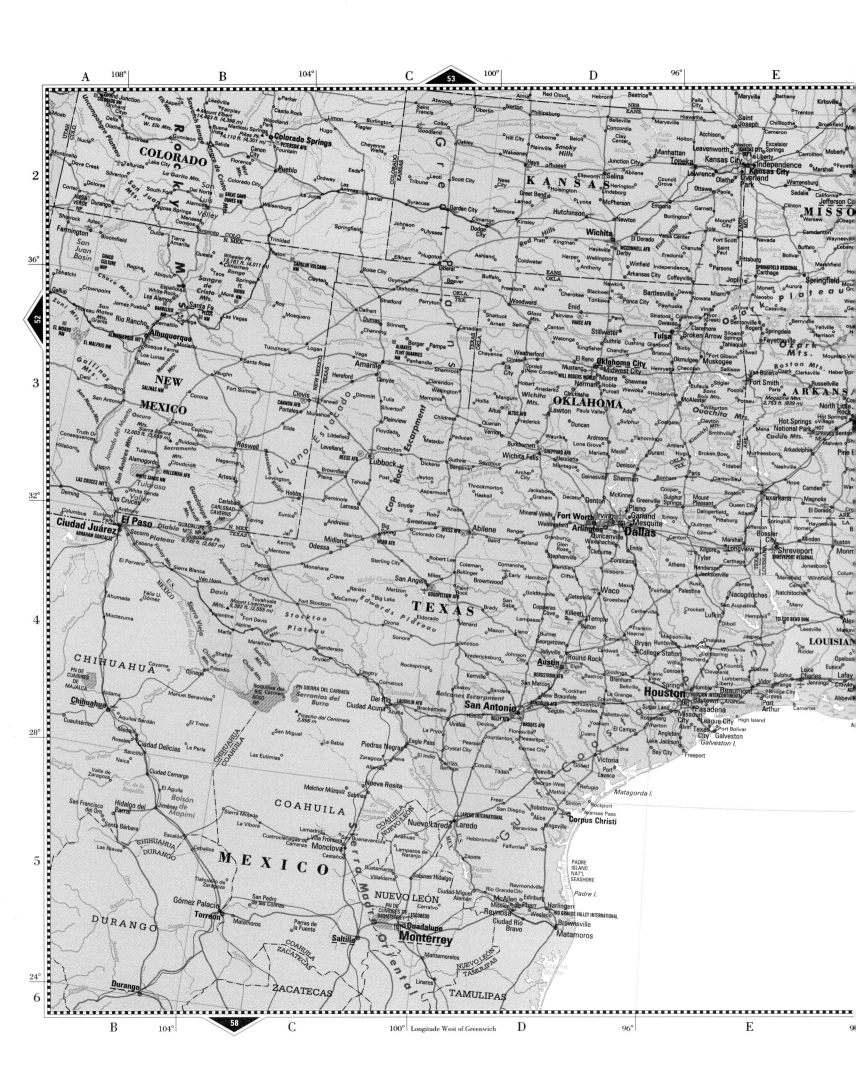

Southeastern United States

POPULATION OF CITIES AND TOWNS

■ OVER 2,000,000   ● 500,000 - 999,999   ● 100,000 - 249,999   ◦ 10,000 - 29,999
□ 1,000,000 - 1,999,999   ● 250,000 - 499,999   ◦ 30,000 - 99,999   · UNDER 10,000

SCALE 1:7,000,000   LAMBERT CONFORMAL CONIC PROJECTION

MILES 0   100   200   300
KILOMETERS 0   100   200   300

Middle America and Caribbean

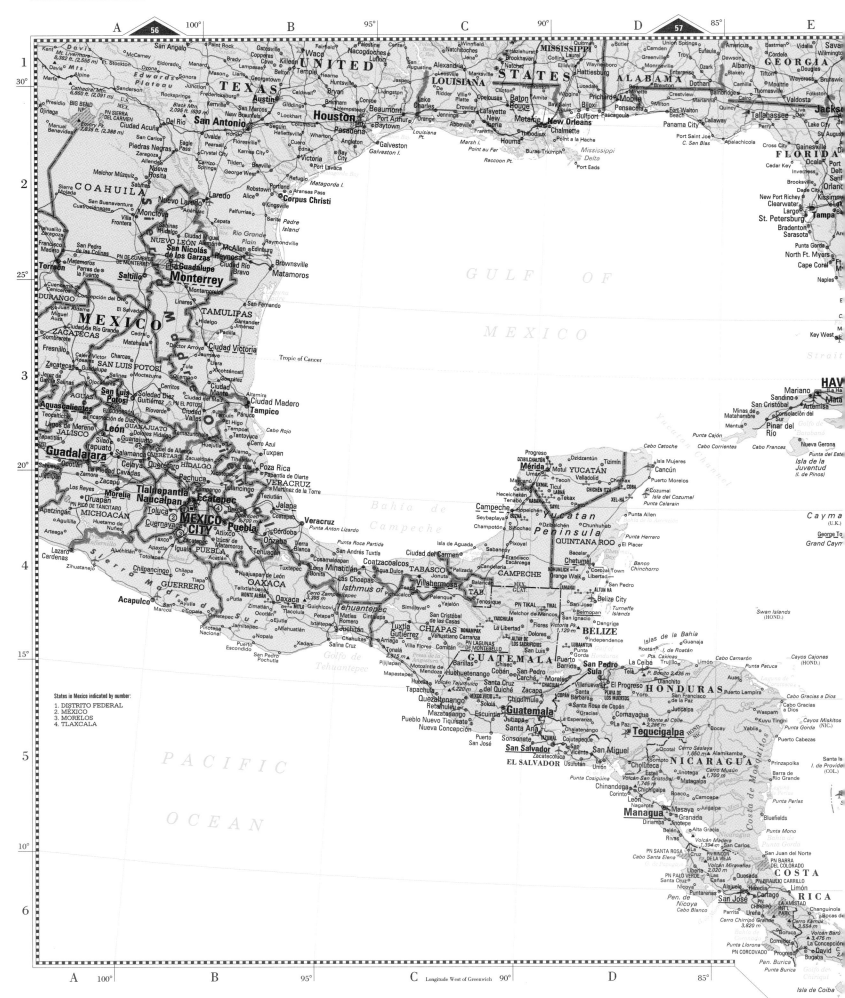

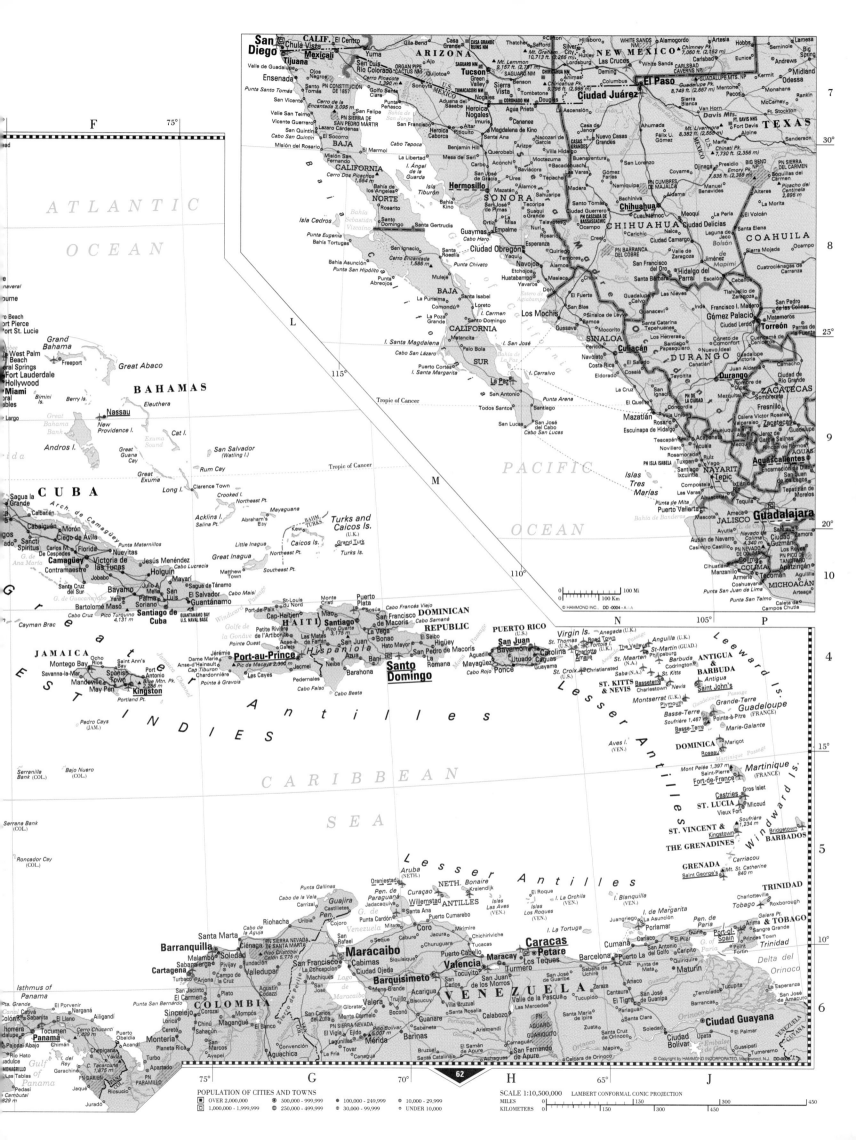

South America - Physical

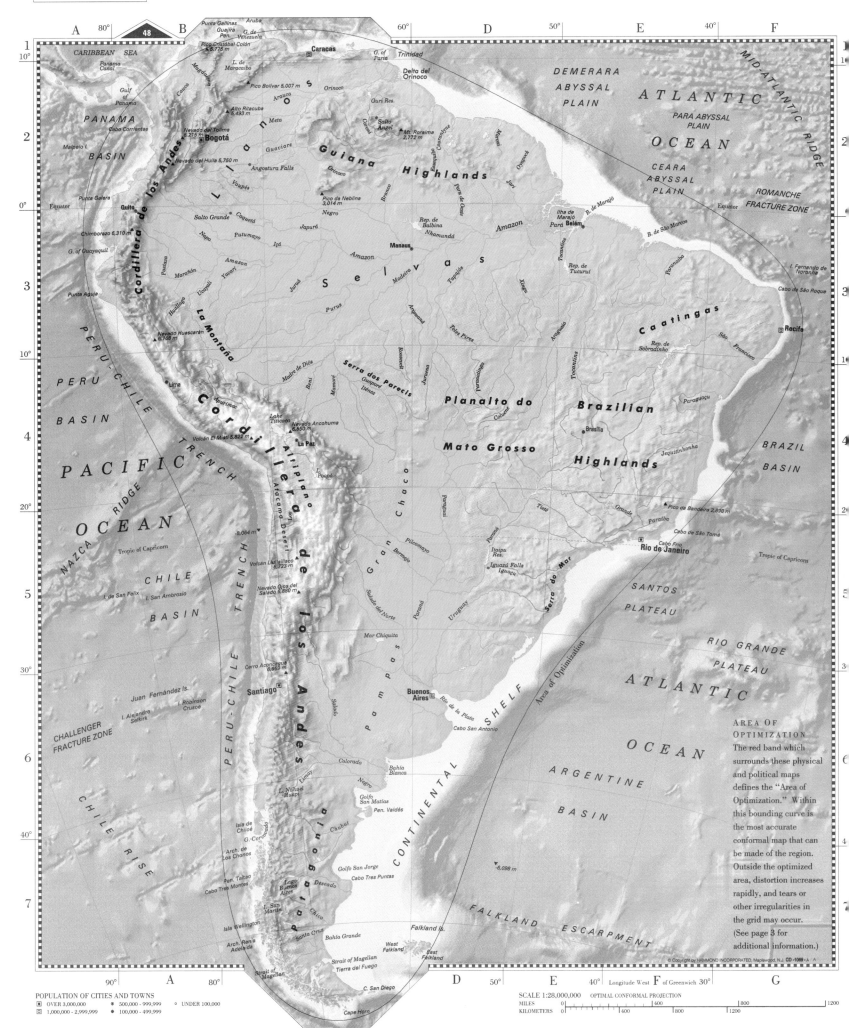

48

CARIBBEAN SEA

Panama Canal

Gulf of Panama

PANAMA

Malpelo I.

Cabo Corrientes

BASIN

Punta Galera

Equator

Quito

Chimborazo 6,310 m

G. of Guayaquil

Punta Aguja

Punta Gallinas
Guajira Pen.
Aruba
G. de Venezuela
Pico Cristóbal Colón 5,775 m
L. de Maracaibo
Pico Bolívar 5,007 m
Alto Ritacuba 5,493 m
Nevado del Tolima 5,215 m
Bogotá
Nevado del Huila 5,750 m
Angostura Falls

Caracas
G. of Paria
Trinidad

Delta del Orinoco

Orinoco
Guri Res.
Salto Angel
Mt. Roraima 2,772 m

DEMERARA ABYSSAL PLAIN

PARA ABYSSAL PLAIN

ATLANTIC

OCEAN

CEARA ABYSSAL PLAIN

ROMANCHE FRACTURE ZONE

MID-ATLANTIC RIDGE

L l a n o s

Cabo Corrientes

Cauca
Magdalena
Meta
Arauca
Guaviare

Cordillera de los Andes

Voupés

Napo
Pastaza
Marañón

Salto Grande
Caquetá
Putumayo
Içá
Yavari
Ucayali
Huallaga

La Montaña

Nevado Huascarán 6,768 m

Lima

Apurímac

Orinoco
Negro

Pico da Neblina 3,014 m

Guiana Highlands

Branco

Puru de Oeste

Amazon

Rep. de Balbina
Nhamundá

Japurá
Juruá
Purus

S e l v a s

Amazon

Manaus

Madeira
Tapajós
Xingu

Rep. de Tucuruí

Ilha de Marajó
Pará
Belém
B. de Marajó
B. de São Marcos

Equator

Parnaíba

I. Fernando de Noronha

Cabo de São Roque

Recife

Mirim
Essequibo
Courantyne
Oyapoc

Jari
Tocantins
Araguaia
Tocantins

São Francisco

Caatingas

Rep. de Sobradinho

PERU-CHILE

PERU

BASIN

Cordillera

Madre de Dios
Beni
Mamoré
Guaporé
Iténez

Roosevelt
Juruena

Teles Pires

Serra dos Parecis

Planalto do

Mato Grosso

Brazilian

Highlands

Brasília

Jequitinhonha

Paraguaçu

BRAZIL

BASIN

PACIFIC

OCEAN

NAZCA

RIDGE

CHILE

BASIN

I. de San Félix
I. San Ambrosio

Tropic of Capricorn

CHALLENGER FRACTURE ZONE

Lake Titicaca
Nevado Ancohuma 6,550 m
La Paz
Volcán El Misti 5,822 m
Altiplano
Atacama Desert
-8,064 m
Volcán Llullaillaco 6,723 m
Nevado Ojos del Salado 6,880 m

L. Poopó

Cordillera de los Andes

Gran Chaco

Pilcomayo
Bermejo

Salado del Norte

Paraguay
Paraná
Tietê
Paraná
Uruguay

Itaipu Res.
Iguazú Falls
Iguaçu

Serra do Mar

Columbi

Grande
Paraná

Pico da Bandeira 2,890 m

Cabo de São Tomé
Cabo Frio
Rio de Janeiro

SANTOS PLATEAU

Tropic of Capricorn

RIO GRANDE PLATEAU

ATLANTIC

OCEAN

Cerro Aconcagua 6,959 m
Santiago

Juan Fernández Is.
I. Alejandro Selkirk
I. Robinson Crusoe

PERU-CHILE TRENCH

Salado

Mar Chiquita

P a m p a s

Colorado
Negro

Rto de la Plata
Buenos Aires

Cabo San Antonio

CONTINENTAL SHELF

Area of Optimization

ARGENTINE

BASIN

Bahía Blanca

CHILE

RISE

Isla de Chiloé
G. Corcovado
Arch. de Los Chonos
Pen. Taitao
Cabo Tres Montes

L. Nahuel Huapi

Limay

Golfo San Matías
Pen. Valdés

Chubut

Golfo San Jorge
Cabo Tres Puntas

-6,098 m

FALKLAND

ESCARPMENT

Lago Buenos Aires
Deseado

P a t a g o n i a

Chico
Santa Cruz
Bahía Grande

Falkland Is.

West Falkland
East Falkland

Isla Wellington
Arch. Reina Adelaida
Strait of Magellan
Tierra del Fuego

C. San Diego

Cape Horn

AREA OF OPTIMIZATION. The red band which surrounds these physical and political maps defines the "Area of Optimization." Within this bounding curve is the most accurate conformal map that can be made of the region. Outside the optimized area, distortion increases rapidly, and tears or other irregularities in the grid may occur. (See page 3 for additional information.)

POPULATION OF CITIES AND TOWNS

◼ OVER 3,000,000
◻ 1,000,000 - 2,999,999
● 500,000 - 999,999
◉ 100,000 - 499,999
○ UNDER 100,000

SCALE 1:28,000,000 OPTIMAL CONFORMAL PROJECTION

MILES 0 400 800
KILOMETERS 0 400 800 1200

Longitude West F of Greenwich 30°

South America - Political

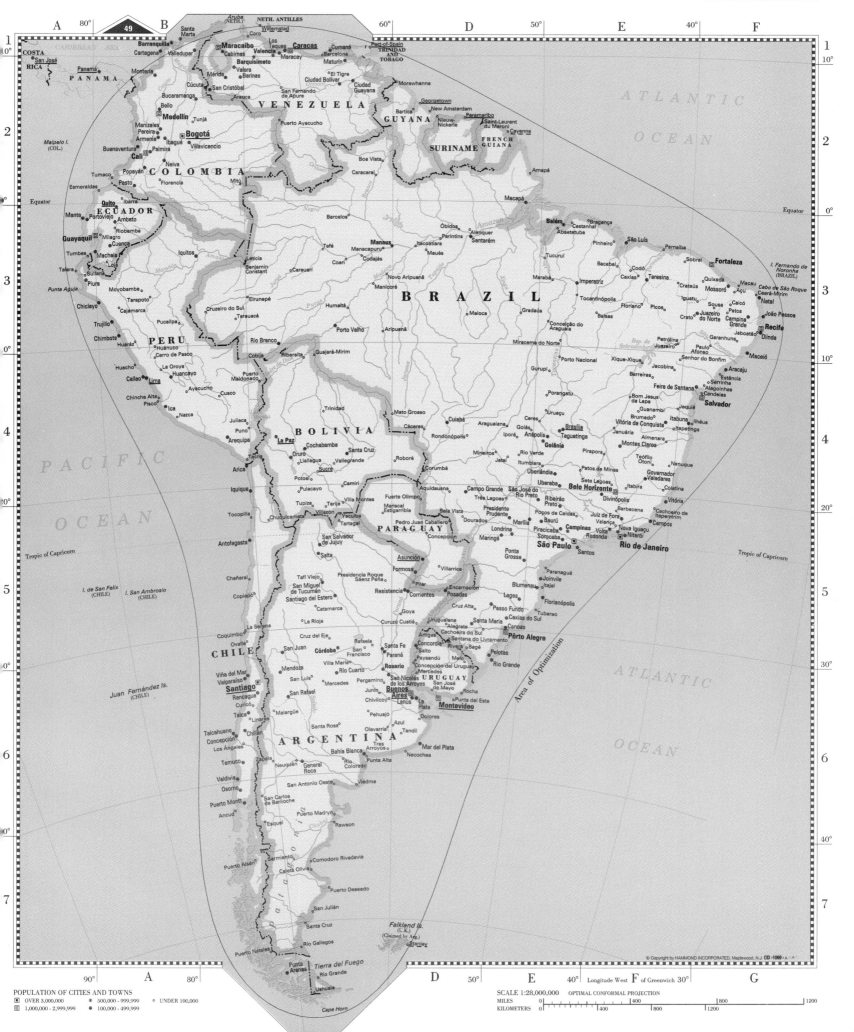

Northern South America

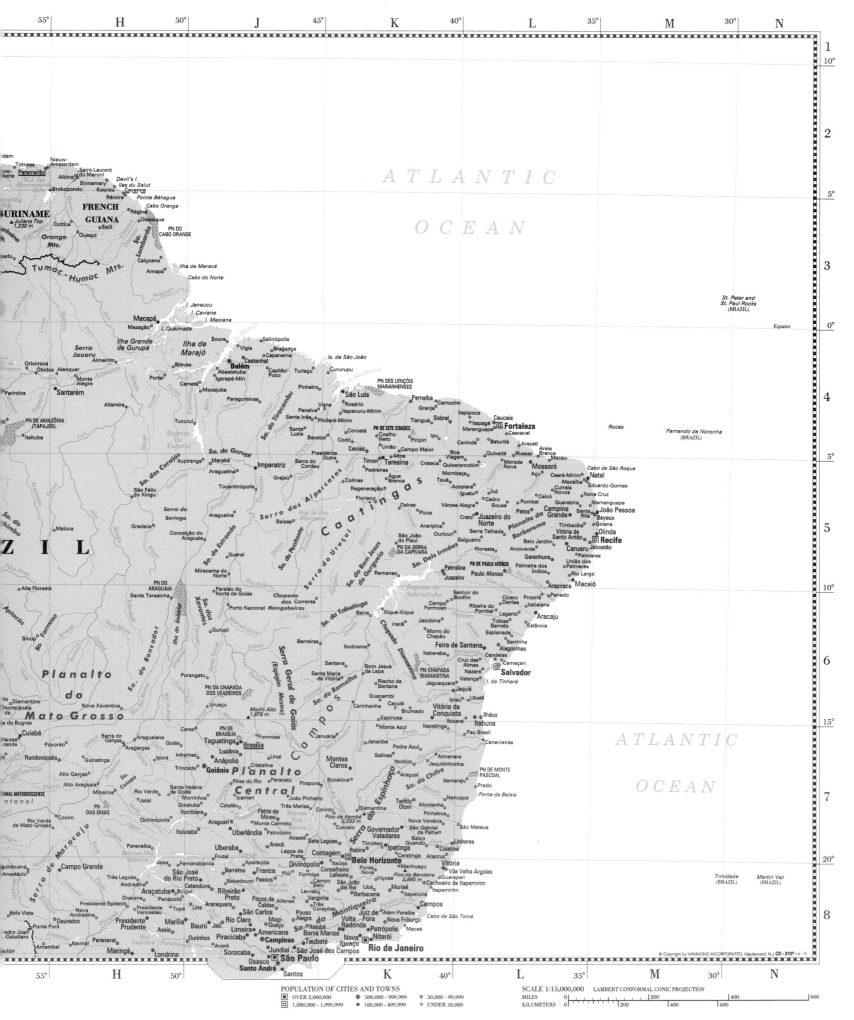

ATLANTIC

OCEAN

SURINAME

FRENCH GUIANA

▲ Juliana Top 1,230 m

Orange Mts.

Tumuc-Humac Mts.

Paramaribo
Nieuw-Amsterdam
Totness
Albina
Saint-Laurent du Maroni
Sinnamary
Kourou
Cayenne
Devil's I.
Iles du Salut
Rémire
Régina
Cabo Orange
Oiapoque
Saül
Ouaqui
Calçoene

PN DO CABO ORANGE

BRAZIL

Amapá
Macapá
Mazagão
I. Janaucu
I. Caviana
I. Mexiana
I. Queimada

Serra Jauaru

Ilha Grande de Gurupá

Ilha de Marajó

Breves
Portel
Cametá
Soure
Salinópolis
Vigia
Capanema
Bragança
Castanhal
Belém
Abaetetuba
Igarapé-Miri
Mocajuba
Capitão Poço
Turiaçu
Cururupu

Santarém
Monte Alegre
Óbidos
Alenquer
Oriximiná
Almeirim

Altamira
Itaituba

PN DE AMAZÔNIA (TAPAJÓS)

Paragominas
Tucuruí
Sa. do Tiracambu
Sa. do Gurupi

Pinheiro
Viana
Penalva
Santa Inês
Pindaré-Mirim
São Luís
Rosário
Itapecuru-Mirim
Coroatá
Santa Luzia
Bacabal
Codó
Caxias

PN DES LENÇÓIS MARANHENSES

Parnaíba
Camocim
Granja
Tutóia
Tianguá
Sobral
Ipu
Piripiri
Campo Maior
Coelho Neto
União

Teresina
Timon
Pedreiras
Barra do Corda

Imperatriz
Marabá
Araguatins
Tocantinópolis
Grajaú
Colinas
Regeneração
Floriano
Balsas

Serra da Seringa

Sa. dos Carajás

São Félix do Xingu
Itupiranga

Araguaína
Gradaús
Conceição do Araguaia

Sa. do Estrondo

Serra das Alpercatas

Caatingas

Oeiras
Picos
Araripina
Ouricuri
PN DA SERRA DA CAPIVARA

São João do Piauí
Remanso

Sa. do Uruçuí

Sa. do Bom Jesus do Gurguéia

Sa. Dois Irmãos

Petrolina
Juazeiro

Itapagé
Maranguape
Fortaleza
Baturité
Caucaia
Canindé
Quixadá
Russas
Aracati
Areia Branca
Macau

Boa Viagem
Crateús
Quixeramobim
Mombaça
Tauá
Acopiara
Iguatu
Icó
Cedro

Morada Nova
Mossoró
Açu
Ceará-Mirim
Macaíba
Natal
Currais Novos
Calçó
Nova Cruz
Eduardo Gomes

Rocas (BRAZIL)

Fernando de Noronha (BRAZIL)

Várzea Alegre
Crato
Juazeiro do Norte
Serra Talhada
Salgueiro
Floresta
Arcoverde

Pombal
Patos
Guarabira
Campina Grande
Santa Rita
João Pessoa
Timbaúba
Vitória de Santo Antão
Belo Jardim
Caruaru
Recife
Olinda
Jaboatão

Cabo de São Roque

Planalto da Borborema

Garanhuns
Bayeux
Goiana

Mamanguape

PN DE PAULO AFONSO
Paulo Afonso
Palmeira dos Índios
União dos Palmares
Palmares
Rio Largo
Arapiraca
Maceió
Penedo

Planalto do Mato Grosso

Diamantino
Nortelândia
Cuiabá

Alta Floresta
Nova Xavantina

Sa. do Roncador

Ilha do Bananal

PN DO ARAGUAIA

Santa Teresinha
Paraíso do Norte de Goiás
Porto Nacional

Chapada das Mangabeiras

Sa. da Tabatinga

Correntes
Barra

Xique-Xique
Irecê
Jacobina

Senhor do Bonfim
Campo Formoso

Chapada Diamantina

Ribeira do Pombal
Cícero Dantas
Propriá
Itabaiana

Jeremoabo
Tobias Barreto
Lagarto
Aracaju
Estância

Esplanada
Serrinha
Alagoinhas
Candeias

Sobradinho

Repressa de Sobradinho

Morro do Chapéu
Ibotirama

Barreiras
Santana

Bom Jesus da Lapa
Riacho de Santana
Santa Maria da Vitória

Feira de Santana
Itaberaba
PN CHAPADA DIAMANTINA
Cruz das Almas
Nazaré
Camaçari
Salvador
I. de Tinharé

Jaguaquara
Valença

Porangatu
Uruaçu
Ceres
Formosa
Goiás
Inhumas
Iporá

Morro Alto 1,678 m

Sa. do Ramalho

Campos

Sa. Geral de Goiás

(Espigão Mestre)

Guanambi
Caculé
Carinhanha
Brumado
Espinosa

Vitória da Conquista
Ipiaú
Ubatã
Jequié
Ilhéus
Itabuna
Ibicaraí

Guaratinga
Itapetinga

Rondonópolis

PN DE BRASÍLIA
Taguatinga
Brasília
Luziânia
Cristalina
Formosa
Unaí

Monte Azul
Janaúba
Salinas

Itapetinga
Canavieiras

PN DA CHAPADA DOS VEADEIROS

Pau Brasil

ATLANTIC

OCEAN

Anápolis
Trindade
Goiânia

Planalto Central

Montes Claros

Pedra Azul
Itaobim
Almenara
Jequitinhonha

Pirapora
Bocaiúva

Araçuaí

PN DE MONTE PASCOAL

Prado
Itamaraju
Ponta de Baleia

Pico da Ibiapina

Ipameri
Pires do Rio
Paracatu
Catalão
Goiatuba
Itumbiara

Sa. do Chifre

Araguari
Uberlândia
João Pinheiro
Patos de Minas
Monte Carmelo
Patrocínio

Três Marias
Corinto
Curvelo

Diamantina
PN DAS EMAS

Pico do Itambé 2,033 m

Teófilo Otoni
Montanha
Nanuque
São Mateus

Sa. Espinhaço

Serra do Espinhaço

Pinheiros
Nova Venécia
Pancas
Linhares

Coxim
Rio Verde de Mato Grosso

Jataí
Mineiros
Quirinópolis

Rio Verde
Santa Helena de Goiás
Morrinhos

Abaeté
Sete Lagoas
Paraopeba

São Gonçalo
São Gabriel da Palha
Baixo Guandu
Colatina
Aracruz

Serra do Mar

Araxá
Uberaba
Frutal

Araguari
Curvelo
Timóteo
Governador Valadares
Ipatinga
Caratinga

Vitória
Vila Velha
Argolas

Paranaíba
Campo Grande
Três Lagoas

Aparecida
Barretos
Frutal
Ituiutaba

Patrocínio
Lagoa da Prata
Divinópolis
Contagem
Belo Horizonte
Conselheiro Lafaiete
Ponte Nova
Manhuaçu

Viçosa
Muriaé
Itaperuna
Cachoeiro de Itapemirim

Pico da Bandeira 2,890 m

PN DO ITATIAIA

Trinidade (BRAZIL)
Martin Vaz (BRAZIL)

Andradina
Araçatuba
Catanduva
São José do Rio Preto
Penápolis
Birigui
Dracena
Lins
Araraquara

São Carlos
Ribeirão Preto
Piracicaba

Piuí
Campo Belo
Formiga
Lavras
Passos
São João del Rei
Poços de Caldas
Alfenas
Varginha
Três Corações

Além Paraíba
Juiz de Fora
Nova Friburgo
Campos
Macaé

Cabo de São Tomé

Presidente Epitácio
Presidente Prudente
Marília
Bauru
Jaú
Mogi-Guaçu
Americana
Campinas
Limeira
Rio Claro
São José dos Campos
Taubaté
Pouso Alegre

Sa. da Mantiqueira

Barra Mansa
Volta Redonda
Resende
Nova Iguaçu
Rio de Janeiro
Niterói
Petrópolis

Assis
Ourinhos
Avaré
Sorocaba
Jundiaí
Osasco
São Paulo
Santo André
Santos

Maringá
Londrina

POPULATION OF CITIES AND TOWNS

■ OVER 2,000,000
□ 1,000,000 - 1,999,999
◉ 500,000 - 999,999
◉ 100,000 - 499,999
○ 50,000 - 99,999
○ UNDER 50,000

SCALE 1:15,000,000 LAMBERT CONFORMAL CONIC PROJECTION

MILES 0 — 200 — 400 — 600
KILOMETERS 0 — 200 — 400 — 600

© Copyright by HAMMOND INCORPORATED, Maplewood, N.J. CD • 2107 • A • A

Southern South America

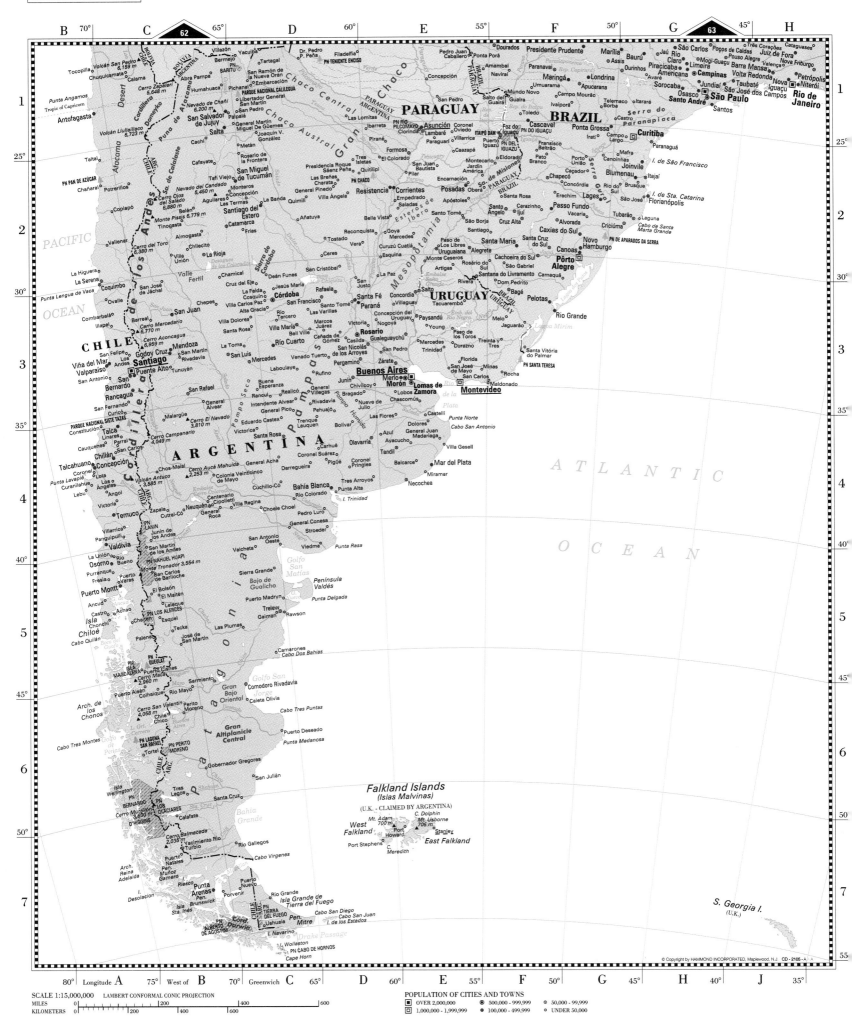

SCALE 1:15,000,000   LAMBERT CONFORMAL CONIC PROJECTION

MILES 0   200   400   600

KILOMETERS 0   200   400   600

POPULATION OF CITIES AND TOWNS

- ■ OVER 2,000,000
- ▣ 1,000,000 - 1,999,999
- ● 500,000 - 999,999
- ● 100,000 - 499,999
- ● 50,000 - 99,999
- ○ UNDER 50,000

© Copyright by HAMMOND INCORPORATED, Maplewood, N.J.   CD - 2105 - A - A

Index of the World

This index is a comprehensive listing of the places and geographic features found in the atlas. Names are arranged in strict alphabetical order, without regard to hyphens or spaces. Every name is followed by the country or area to which it belongs. Except for cities, towns, countries and cultural areas, all entries include a reference to feature type, such as province, river, island, peak, and so on. The page number and alpha-numeric code appear in blue to the left of each listing. The page number directs you to the largest scale map on which the name can be found. The code refers to the grid squares formed by the horizontal and vertical lines of latitude and longitude on each map. Following the letters from left to right and the numbers from top to bottom helps you to locate quickly the square containing the place or feature. Inset maps have their own alpha-numeric codes. Names that are accompanied by a point symbol are indexed to the symbol's location on the map. Other names are indexed to the initial letter of the name. When a map name contains a subordinate or alternate name, both names are listed in the index. To conserve space and provide room for more entries, many abbreviations are used in this index. The primary abbreviations are listed below.

Index Abbreviations

A Ab,Can	Alberta	**Cap. Terr.**	Capital Territory	**Gha.**	Ghana	**Me,US**	Maine
Acad.	Academy	Cay.	Cayman Islands	Gib.	Gibraltar	Mem.	Memorial
ACT	Australian Capital Territory	C.G.	Coast Guard	Glac.	Glacier	Mex.	Mexico
		Chan.	Channel	Gov.	Governorate	Mi,US	Michigan
A.F.B.	Air Force Base	Chl.	Channel Islands	Govt.	Government	Micr.	Micronesia, Federated States of
Afld.	Airfield	Co.	County	Gre.	Greece		
Afg.	Afghanistan	Co,US	Colorado	Grld.	Greenland	Mil.	Military
Afr.	Africa	Col.	Colombia	Gren.	Grenada	Mn,US	Minnesota
Ak,US	Alaska	Com.	Comoros	Grsld.	Grassland	Mo,US	Missouri
Al,US	Alabama	Cont.	Continent	Guad.	Guadeloupe	Mol.	Moldova
Alb.	Albania	CpV.	Cape Verde Islands	Guat.	Guatemala	Mon.	Monument
Alg.	Algeria			Gui.	Guinea	Mona.	Monaco
Amm. Dep.	Ammunition Depot	CR	Costa Rica	Guy.	Guyana	Mong.	Mongolia
		Cr.	Creek			Monts.	Montserrat
And.	Andorra	Cro.	Croatia	**H** Har.	Harbor	Mor.	Morocco
Ang.	Angola	CSea.	Coral Sea Islands Territory	Hi,US	Hawaii	Moz.	Mozambique
Angu.	Anguilla			Hist.	Historic(al)	Mrsh.	Marshall Islands
Ant.	Antarctica	Ct,US	Connecticut	HK	Hong Kong		
Anti.	Antigua and Barbuda	Ctr.	Center	Hon.	Honduras	Mrta.	Mauritania
		Ctry.	Country	Hts.	Heights	Mrts.	Mauritius
Ar,US	Arkansas	Cyp.	Cyprus	Hun.	Hungary	Ms,US	Mississippi
Arch.	Archipelago	Czh.	Czech Republic			Mt.	Mount
Arg.	Argentina			**I** Ia,US	Iowa	Mt,US	Montana
Arm.	Armenia	**D** DC,US	District of Columbia	Ice.	Iceland	Mtn., Mts.	Mountain, Mountains
Arpt.	Airport			Id,US	Idaho		
Aru.	Aruba	De,US	Delaware	Il,US	Illinois	Mun. Arpt.	Municipal Airport
ASam.	American Samoa	Den.	Denmark	IM	Isle of Man		
Ash.	Ashmore and Cartier Islands	Depr.	Depression	In,US	Indiana	**N** NAm.	North America
		Dept.	Department	Ind. Res.	Indian Reservation	Namb.	Namibia
Aus.	Austria	Des.	Desert			NAnt.	Netherlands Antilles
Austl.	Australia	DF	Distrito Federal	Indo.	Indonesia		
Aut.	Autonomous	Dist.	District	Int'l	International	Nat'l	National
Az,US	Arizona	Djib.	Djibouti	Ire.	Ireland	Nav.	Naval
Azer.	Azerbaijan	Dom.	Dominica	Isl., Isls.	Island, Islands	NB,Can	New Brunswick
Azor.	Azores	Dpcy.	Dependency	Isr.	Israel	Nbrhd.	Neighborhood
		DRep.	Dominican Republic	Isth.	Isthmus	NC,US	North Carolina
B Bahm.	Bahamas			It.	Italy	NCal.	New Caledonia
Bahr.	Bahrain	**E** Ecu.	Ecuador	IvC.	Ivory Coast	ND,US	North Dakota
Bang.	Bangladesh	Emb.	Embankment			Ne,US	Nebraska
Bar.	Barbados	Eng.	Engineering	**J** Jam.	Jamaica	Neth.	Netherlands
BC,Can	British Columbia	Eng,UK	England	Jor.	Jordan	Nf,Can	Newfoundland
Bela.	Belarus	EqG.	Equatorial Guinea			Nga.	Nigeria
Belg.	Belgium			**K** Kaz.	Kazakhstan	NH,US	New Hampshire
Belz.	Belize	Erit..	Eritrea	Kiri.	Kiribati	NI,UK	Northern Ireland
Ben.	Benin	ESal.	El Salvador	Ks,US	Kansas	Nic.	Nicaragua
Berm.	Bermuda	Est.	Estonia	Kuw.	Kuwait	NJ,US	New Jersey
Bfld.	Battlefield	Eth.	Ethiopia	Ky,US	Kentucky	NKor.	North Korea
Bhu.	Bhutan	Eur.	Europe	Kyr.	Kyrgyzstan	NM,US	New Mexico
Bol.	Bolivia					NMar.	Northern Mariana Islands
Bor.	Borough	**F** Falk.	Falkland Islands	**L** La,US	Louisiana		
Bosn.	Bosnia and Hercegovina			Lab.	Laboratory	Nor.	Norway
		Far.	Faroe Islands	Lag.	Lagoon	NS,Can	Nova Scotia
Bots.	Botswana	Fed. Dist.	Federal District	Lakesh.	Lakeshore	Nv,US	Nevada
Braz.	Brazil	Fin.	Finland	Lat.	Latvia	NW,Can	Northwest Territories
Brln.	British Indian Ocean Territory	Fl,US	Florida	Lcht.	Liechtenstein		
		For.	Forest	Ldg.	Landing	NY,US	New York
Bru.	Brunei	Fr.	France	Leb.	Lebanon	NZ	New Zealand
Bul.	Bulgaria	FrAnt.	French Southern and Antarctic Lands	Les.	Lesotho		
Burk.	Burkina			Libr.	Liberia	**O** Obl.	Oblast
Buru.	Burundi			Lith.	Lithuania	Oh,US	Ohio
BVI	British Virgin Islands	FrG.	French Guiana	Lux.	Luxembourg	Ok,US	Oklahoma
		FrPol.	French Polynesia			On,Can	Ontario
C Ca,US	California			**M** Ma,US	Massachusetts	Or,US	Oregon
CAfr.	Central African Republic	**G** Ga,US	Georgia	Macd.	Macedonia		
		Galp.	Galapagos Islands	Madg.	Madagascar	**P** Pa,US	Pennsylvania
Camb.	Cambodia			Madr.	Madeira	PacUS	Pacific Islands, U.S.
Camr.	Cameroon	Gam.	Gambia	Malay.	Malaysia		
Can.	Canada	Gaza	Gaza Strip	Mald.	Maldives	Pak.	Pakistan
Can.	Canal	GBis.	Guinea-Bissau	Malw.	Malawi	Pan.	Panama
Canl.	Canary Islands	Geo.	Georgia	Mart.	Martinique	Par.	Paraguay
Cap.	Capital	Ger.	Germany	May.	Mayotte	Par.	Parish
Cap. Dist.	Capital District			Mb,Can	Manitoba		
				Md,US	Maryland		

PE,Can	Prince Edward Island	**Sval.**	Svalbard
Pen.	Peninsula	Swaz.	Swaziland
Phil.	Philippines	Swe.	Sweden
Phys. Reg.	Physical Region	Swi.	Switzerland
Pitc.	Pitcairn Islands	**T** Tah.	Tahiti
Plat.	Plateau	Tai.	Taiwan
PNG	Papua New Guinea	Taj.	Tajikistan
		Tanz.	Tanzania
Pol.	Poland	Ter.	Terrace
Port.	Portugal	Terr.	Territory
Poss.	Possession	Thai.	Thailand
Pkwy.	Parkway	Tn,US	Tennessee
PR	Puerto Rico	Tok.	Tokelau
Pref.	Prefecture	Trg.	Training
Prov.	Province	Trin.	Trinidad and Tobago
Prsv.	Preserve		
Pt.	Point	Trkm.	Turkmenistan
		Trks.	Turks and Caicos Islands
Q Qu,Can	Quebec		
		Tun.	Tunisia
R Rec.	Recreation(al)	Tun.	Tunnel
Ref.	Refuge	Turk.	Turkey
Reg.	Region	Tuv.	Tuvalu
Rep.	Republic	Twp.	Township
Res.	Reservoir, Reservation	Tx,US	Texas
Reun.	Réunion	**U** UAE	United Arab Emirates
RI,US	Rhode Island		
Riv.	River	Ugan.	Uganda
Rom.	Romania	UK	United Kingdom
Rsv.	Reserve	Ukr.	Ukraine
Rus.	Russia	Uru.	Uruguay
Rvwy.	Riverway	US	United States
Rwa.	Rwanda	USVI	U.S. Virgin Islands
S SAfr.	South Africa	Ut,US	Utah
SAm.	South America	Uzb.	Uzbekistan
SaoT.	São Tomé and Príncipe	**V** Va,US	Virginia
		Val.	Valley
SAr.	Saudi Arabia	Van.	Vanuatu
Sc,UK	Scotland	VatC.	Vatican City
SC,US	South Carolina	Ven.	Venezuela
SD,US	South Dakota	Viet.	Vietnam
Seash.	Seashore	Vill.	Village
Sen.	Senegal	Vol.	Volcano
Sey.	Seychelles	Vt,US	Vermont
SGeo.	South Georgia and Sandwich Islands	**W** Wa,US	Washington
		Wal,UK	Wales
Sing.	Singapore	Wall.	Wallis and Futuna
Sk,Can	Saskatchewan		
SKor.	South Korea	WBnk.	West Bank
SLeo.	Sierra Leone	Wi,US	Wisconsin
Slov.	Slovenia	Wild.	Wildlife, Wilderness
Slvk.	Slovakia		
SMar.	San Marino	WSah.	Western Sahara
Sol.	Solomon Islands	WSam.	Western Samoa
Som.	Somalia	WV,US	West Virginia
Sp.	Spain	Wy,US	Wyoming
Spr., Sprs.	Spring, Springs		
SrL.	Sri Lanka	**Y** Yem.	Yemen
Sta.	Station	Yk,Can	Yukon Territory
StH.	Saint Helena	Yugo.	Yugoslavia
Str.	Strait		
StK.	Saint Kitts and Nevis	**Z** Zam.	Zambia
StL.	Saint Lucia	Zim.	Zimbabwe
StP.	Saint Pierre and Miquelon		
StV.	Saint Vincent and the Grenadines		
Sur.	Suriname		

67
Canto – Furna

47/H5 Canton (isl.), Kiri.
54/D3 Canton, Oh,US
30/B3 Canton (Guangzhou), China
52/E3 Canyonlands Nat'l Pk., Ut,US
55/J2 Cape Breton (isl.), NS,Can
57/H5 Cape Coral, Fl,US
57/F2 Cape Girardeau, Mo,US
42/C7 Cape Town (cap.), SAfr.
14/H5 Cape Verde
45/D2 Cape York (pen.), Austl.
59/G4 Cap-Haïtien, Haiti
63/J4 Capim (riv.), Braz.
52/E3 Capitol Reef Nat'l Pk., Ut,US
63/H8 Capivara (res.), Braz.
42/D4 Caprivi Strip (reg.), Namb.
62/D4 Caquetá (riv.), Col.
62/E1 Caracas (cap.), Ven.
63/H5 Carajás (mts.), Braz.
54/B4 Carbondale, Il,US
20/D3 Carcassonne, Fr.
18/D4 Cardiff (cap.), Wal,UK
18/C3 Cardigan (bay), Wal,UK
59/G4 Caribbean (sea)
50/C2 Cariboo (mts.), BC,Can
55/G2 Caribou, Me,US
18/D3 Carlisle, Eng,UK
54/E3 Carlisle, Pa,US
18/C3 Carlow, Ire.
53/F4 Carlsbad, NM,US
53/F4 Carlsbad Caverns Nat'l Pk., NM,US
59/H4 Carolina, PR
46/D4 Caroline (isls.), Micr.
19/J4 Carpathians (mts.), Eur.
45/C2 Carpentaria (gulf), Austl.
21/F2 Carrara, It.
52/C3 Carson (sink), Nv,US
52/C3 Carson City (cap.), Nv,US
62/C1 Cartagena, Col.
20/C4 Cartagena, Sp.
58/E6 Cartago, CR
40/D1 Casablanca, Mor.
52/E4 Casa Grande, Az,US
50/C5 Cascade (range), US
64/F1 Cascavel, Braz.
50/G5 Casper, Wy,US
24/F6 Caspian (sea)
20/D3 Castellón de la Plana, Sp.
59/J5 Castries (cap.), StL.
20/D3 Catalonia (reg.), Sp.
21/G4 Catania, It.
21/H4 Catanzaro, It.
32/B3 Catherine (mt.), Egypt
55/F3 Catskill (mts.), NY,US
23/F5 Caucasus (mts.), Eur.
63/J3 Caviana (isl.), Braz.
34/D2 Cawnpore (Kanpur), India
63/K4 Caxias, Braz.
64/F2 Caxias do Sul, Braz.
62/G3 Cayambe (mtn.), Ecu.
63/H3 Cayenne (cap.), FrG.
58/E4 Cayman Islands, UK
30/D5 Cebu, Phil.
52/D3 Cedar City, Ut,US
53/J2 Cedar Falls, Ia,US
53/K2 Cedar Rapids, Ia,US
59/L8 Cedros (isl.), Mex.
37/F3 Celebes (sea), Asia
37/E4 Celebes (isl.), Indo.
18/C4 Celtic (sea), Eur.
37/H4 Cenderawasih (bay), Indo.
41/J6 Central African Republic
62/C5 Central, Cordillera (mts.), SAm.
54/B4 Centralia, Il,US
50/C4 Centralia, Wa,US
33/H3 Central Makrān (mts.), Pak.
63/J7 Central, Planalto (plat.), Braz.
25/L2 Central Siberian (plat.), Rus.
37/G4 Ceram (isl.), Indo.
37/G4 Ceram (sea), Indo.
64/C4 Cerro Colorados (res.), Arg.
19/H4 České Budějovice, Czh.
20/B5 Ceuta, Sp.
34/D6 Ceylon (isl.)
64/D1 Chaco Austral (reg.), Arg.
62/G8 Chaco Boreal (reg.), Par.
64/D1 Chaco Central (reg.), Arg.
64/D2 Chaco, Gran (reg.), SAm.
64/E2 Chaco Nat'l Park, Arg.
41/J4 Chad
40/H5 Chad (lake), Afr.
27/G10 Chagos (arch.), BrIn.
54/E4 Chambersburg, Pa,US
42/F3 Chambeshi (riv.), Zam.
20/E1 Champagne (reg.), Fr.
54/B3 Champaign, Il,US
54/F2 Champlain (lake), NAm.
62/C5 Chan Chan (ruins), Peru
33/L2 Chandigarh, India
34/C3 Chandrapur, India
29/K3 Changchun, China
30/D3 Changhua, Tai.
27/L6 Chang Jiang (Yangtze) (riv.), China
35/K2 Changsha, China
28/G4 Changzhi, China
29/H5 Changzhou, China
64/C1 Chañi (mtn.), Arg.
52/C4 Channel (isls.), Ca,US
45/D3 Channel Country (reg.), Austl.
18/D4 Channel Islands, UK
63/K6 Chapada Diamantina Nat'l Park, Braz.
63/J6 Chapada dos Veadeiros Nat'l Park, Braz.
57/J3 Chapel Hill, NC,US
24/G6 Chardzhou, Trkm.
40/J5 Chari (riv.), Afr.
18/F4 Charleroi, Belg.
57/J3 Charleston, SC,US
54/D4 Charleston (cap.), WV,US
57/H3 Charlotte, NC,US
59/J4 Charlotte Amalie (cap.), USVI
57/J2 Charlottesville, Va,US
55/J2 Charlottetown (cap.), PE,Can
20/D1 Chartres, Fr.
55/H2 Chatham, NB,Can
57/G4 Chattahoochee (riv.), US
57/G4 Chattahoochee, Fl,US
57/G3 Chattanooga, Tn,US
25/T3 Chaunskaya (bay), Rus.
23/D2 Cheboksary, Rus.
54/C2 Cheboygan, Mi,US
40/E2 Chech, Erg (des.), Alg.
54/E3 Cheektowaga, NY,US
50/C4 Chehalis, Wa,US
29/K5 Cheju, SKor.
29/K5 Cheju (isl.), SKor.
29/K5 Cheju (str.), SKor.
50/C4 Chelan (lake), Wa,US
18/D4 Cheltenham, Eng,UK
24/H4 Chelyabinsk, Rus.
25/L2 Chelyuskina (cape), Rus.
19/H4 Chemnitz, Ger.
29/H3 Chengde, China
28/E5 Chengdu (Chengtu), China
23/C4 Chenovtsy, Ukr.
20/C1 Cherbourg, Fr.
23/E2 Cherepovets, Rus.
23/D4 Cherkassy, Ukr.
23/F5 Cherkessk, Rus.
23/D3 Chernigov, Ukr.
23/C4 Chernovtsy, Ukr.
23/C4 Cherry Hill, NJ,US
25/Q3 Cherskiy (range), Rus.
54/E4 Chesapeake (bay), US
18/D3 Chester, Eng,UK
58/D4 Chetumal, Mex.
53/F2 Cheyenne (riv.), US
53/F2 Cheyenne (cap.), Wy,US
35/G4 Chiang Mai, Thai.
30/D3 Chiayi, Tai.
29/N4 Chiba, Japan
54/C3 Chicago, Il,US
58/D3 Chichén-Itzá (ruins), Mex.
45/A3 Chichester (range), Austl.
53/H4 Chickasha, Ok,US
62/C5 Chiclayo, Peru
64/C5 Chico (riv.), Arg.
52/B3 Chico, Ca,US
54/F3 Chicopee, Ma,US
55/G1 Chicoutimi, Qu,Can
29/H3 Chifeng, China
37/K6 Chifre (mts.), Braz.
59/N8 Chihuahua, Mex.
61/B6 Chile
64/B4 Chillán, Chile
54/D4 Chillicothe, Oh,US
64/A5 Chiloé (isl.), Chile
62/C4 Chimborazo (mtn.), Ecu.
62/C5 Chimbote, Peru
31/A3 Chimkent, Kaz.
27/J6 China, People's Rep. of
30/D3 China, Rep. of (Taiwan)
33/K2 Chiniot, Pak.
24/G5 Chirchik, Uzb.
58/E6 Chiriquí (gulf), Pan.
19/M5 Chişinău (cap.), Mold.
28/G1 Chita, Rus.
35/F3 Chittagong, Bang.
42/D4 Chobe Nat'l Park, Bots.
35/H5 Chon Buri, Thai.
29/K3 Chŏngjin, NKor.
29/K4 Chongju, SKor.
30/A2 Chongqing (Chungking), China
29/K4 Chŏnju, SKor.
64/A6 Chonos (arch.), Arg.
34/D3 Chota Nagur (plat.), India
28/G2 Choybalsan, Mong.
48/Q5 Christchurch, NZ
27/K11 Christmas (isl.), Austl.
64/C5 Chubut (riv.), Arg.
25/U3 Chukchi (pen.), Rus.
25/U3 Chukchi (sea), Rus.
52/C5 Chula Vista, Ca,US
24/J4 Chulym (riv.), Rus.
29/K4 Ch'unch'ŏn, SKor.
49/H4 Churchill, Can.
49/H4 Churchill (riv.), Can.
36/C5 Ciamis, Indo.
36/C5 Cianjur, Indo.
59/E3 Cienfuegos, Cuba
36/C5 Cilacap, Indo.
53/G3 Cimarron (riv.), US
54/C4 Cincinnati, Oh,US
21/F3 Cinto (mt.), Fr.
36/C5 Cirebon, Indo.
58/B4 Citlaltépetl (mt.), Mex.
62/E1 Coro, Ven.
62/F2 Ciudad Bolívar, Ven.
62/F2 Ciudad Guayana, Ven.
59/N7 Ciudad Juárez, Mex.
58/B3 Ciudad Madero, Mex.
59/N8 Ciudad Obregón, Mex.
20/B4 Ciudad Real, Sp.
58/B3 Ciudad Victoria, Mex.
55/F3 Claremont, NH,US
53/J3 Claremore, Ok,US
54/D4 Clarksburg, WV,US
57/F3 Clarksdale, Ms,US
57/G2 Clarksville, Tn,US
18/B4 Clear (cape), Ire.
57/H5 Clearwater, Fl,US
50/D4 Clearwater (mts.), Id,US
20/D2 Clermont-Ferrand, Fr.
55/D3 Cleveland, Oh,US
57/G3 Cleveland, Tn,US
53/K2 Clinton, Ia,US
14/D5 Clipperton (isl.), Fr.
52/C3 Clovis, Ca,US
53/G4 Clovis, NM,US
21/J2 Cluj-Napoca, Rom.
18/C3 Clyde, Firth of (inlet), Sc,UK
50/A2 Coast (mts.), Can.
49/E5 Coast (ranges), US
57/H4 Coastal (plain), US
62/E7 Cochabamaba, Bol.
34/C6 Cochin, India
58/E5 Coco (riv.), Hon., Nic.
27/J11 Cocos (isls.), Austl.
55/G3 Cod (cape), Ma,US
50/F4 Cody, Wy,US
50/D4 Coeur d'Alene, Id,US
53/J3 Coffeyville, Ks,US
34/C5 Coimbatore, India
21/A3 Coimbra, Port.
62/E2 Cojedes (riv.), Ven.
59/P10 Colima, Mex.
56/D4 College Station, Tx,US
20/E1 Colmar, Fr.
18/F4 Cologne (Köln), Ger.
62/D3 Colombia
34/C6 Colombo (cap.), SrL.
59/F6 Colón, Pan.
64/D4 Colorado (riv.), Arg.
52/E3 Colorado (plat.), US
52/D4 Colorado (riv.), US
52/F3 Colorado (state), US
56/D4 Colorado (riv.), Tx,US
53/F3 Colorado Springs, Co,US
50/C2 Columbia (mts.), BC,Can
50/C4 Columbia (riv.), NAm.
53/J3 Columbia, Mo,US
50/D4 Columbia (plat.), Or,Wa,US
57/H3 Columbia (cap.), SC,US
57/G3 Columbia, Tn,US
57/G3 Columbus, Ga,US
54/C4 Columbus, In,US
57/F3 Columbus, Ms,US
54/D4 Columbus (cap.), Oh,US
31/B4 Communism (peak), Taj.
21/F2 Como (lake), It.
64/C6 Comodoro Rivadavia, Arg.
40/E6 Comoe Nat'l Park, IvC.
34/C6 Comorin (cape), India
39/G6 Comoros
21/D1 Compiègne, Fr.
41/C6 Conakry (cap.), Gui.
62/F7 Concepción (lake), Bol.
64/B4 Concepción, Chile
52/B3 Concord, Ca,US
55/G3 Concord (cap.), NH,US
57/H3 Concord, NC,US
30/B3 Conghua, China
32/D4 Congo
39/D5 Congo (riv.), Afr.
41/K7 Congo (basin), Zaire
18/B3 Connacht (reg.), Ire.
55/G2 Connecticut (riv.), US
55/F3 Connecticut (state), US
18/G5 Constance (lake), Eur.
21/L2 Constanta, Rom.
41/G1 Constantine, Alg.
63/K7 Contagem, Braz.
62/C7 Continental (ranges), Ab,BC,Can
53/J4 Conway, Ar,US
45/G7 Cook (mt.), NZ
45/H7 Cook (str.), NZ
47/J6 Cook Islands, NZ
50/B5 Coos Bay, Or,US
19/H2 Copenhagen (cap.), Den.
46/E6 Coral (sea)
57/H5 Coral Gables, Fl,US
45/E2 Coral Sea Is. (terr.), Austl.
57/H5 Coral Springs, Fl,US
62/D3 Cordillera de los Picachos Nat'l Park, Col.
64/D3 Córdoba, Arg.
64/D3 Córdoba (mts.), Arg.
20/B4 Córdoba, Sp.
21/H4 Corfu (Kérkira), Gre.
21/J4 Corinth, Gre.
21/J4 Corinth (gulf), Gre.
18/B4 Cork, Ire.
55/K1 Corner Brook, Nf,Can
54/E3 Corning, NY,US
54/F2 Cornwall, On,Can
34/D5 Coromandel (coast), India
58/E6 Coronado (bay), CR
62/D7 Coropuna (mtn.), Peru
56/D5 Corpus Christi, Tx,US
64/E2 Corrientes, Arg.
21/F3 Corsica (isl.), Fr.
56/D3 Corsicana, Tx,US
54/E3 Cortland, NY,US
23/D5 Çorum, Turk.
63/J7 Corumba (riv.), Braz.
50/C4 Corvallis, Or,US
21/G3 Cosenza, It.
54/D3 Coshocton, Oh,US
58/E5 Costa Rica
20/C1 Cotentin (pen.), Fr.
40/F6 Cotonou, Benin
19/H4 Cottbus, Ger.
53/J2 Council Bluffs, Ia,US
18/D3 Coventry, Eng,UK
54/C4 Covington, Ky,US
58/D3 Cozumel (isl.), Mex.
21/J2 Craiova, Rom.
50/E3 Cranbrook, BC,Can
50/C5 Crater Lake Nat'l Pk., Or,US
54/C3 Crawfordsville, In,US
21/G2 Cres (isl.), Cro.
21/K5 Crete (isl.), Gre.
21/K4 Crete (sea), Gre.
23/D4 Crimea (pen.), Ukr.
40/H8 Cristal (mts.), Gabon
62/D1 Cristóbal Colón (peak), Col.
21/G2 Croatia
37/E5 Crocker (range), Malay.
56/E4 Crowley, La,US
42/C2 Cuango (riv.), Ang.
42/B2 Cuanza (riv.), Ang.
59/F3 Cuba
42/C4 Cubango (riv.), Ang.
62/D2 Cucuta, Col.
62/C4 Cuenca, Ecu.
58/B4 Cuernavaca, Mex.
63/G7 Cuiabá, Braz.
63/H6 Culene (riv.), Braz.
45/D3 Culgoa (riv.), Austl.
59/N9 Culiacán, Mex.
57/G3 Cullman, Al,US
62/F1 Cumaná, Ven.
57/G3 Cumberland (plat.), US
57/G2 Cumberland (riv.), US
54/E4 Cumberland, Md,US
18/D3 Cumbrian (mts.), Eng,UK
59/H5 Curaçao (isl.), NAnt.
64/G2 Curitiba, Braz.
62/D6 Cusco, Peru
34/E3 Cuttack, India
21/K4 Cyclades (isls.), Gre.
32/B1 Cyprus
41/K1 Cyrenaica (reg.), Libya
19/H4 Czech Republic
19/J4 Czestochowa, Pol.

D

21/G3 D'Abruzzo Nat'l Park, It.
34/E4 Dacca (Dhaka) (cap.), Bang.
18/G4 Dachau, Ger.
35/J2 Dafang, China
29/J2 Da Hinggang (mts.), China
46/C2 Daito (isls.), Japan
40/B5 Dakar (cap.), Sen.
35/J5 Da Lat, Viet.
55/H1 Dalhousie, NB,Can
29/J4 Dalian, China
56/D3 Dallas, Tx,US
21/G2 Dalmatia (reg.), Cro.
45/D3 Dalrymple (lake), Austl.
57/G3 Dalton, Ga,US
34/B3 Damān, India
32/B2 Damanhur, Egypt
32/C2 Damascus (cap.), Syria
32/F1 Damavand (mt.), Iran
32/B2 Damietta, Egypt
37/H4 Dampier (str.), Indo.
41/P5 Danakil (reg.), Djib., Eth.
35/E2 Da Nang, Viet.
29/J3 Dandong, China
21/L2 Danube (riv.), Eur.
55/C3 Danville, Il,US
54/E4 Danville, Va,US
29/J2 Daqing, China
34/E2 Darbhanga, India
23/C6 Dardanelles (str.), Turk.
42/G2 Dar es Salaam (cap.), Tanz.
28/F2 Darhan, Mong.
41/G6 Darie (hills), Som.
59/F6 Darien Nat'l Park, Pan.
34/E2 Darjiling, India
45/A4 Darling (range), Austl.
45/D4 Darling (riv.), Austl.
45/D3 Darling Downs (ridge), Austl.
18/D3 Darlington, Eng,UK
18/G4 Darmstadt, Ger.
18/C4 Dartmoor Nat'l Park, Eng,UK
55/J2 Dartmouth, NS,Can
45/C2 Darwin, Austl.
64/B7 Darwin (mts.), Chile
41/N5 Dashen Terara, Ras (peak), Eth.
33/F2 Dasht-e Kavīr (des.), Iran
33/G2 Dasht-e Lūt (des.), Iran
28/G3 Datong, China
19/L2 Daugava (Western Dvina) (riv.), Lat.
19/L3 Daugavpils, Lat.
30/E6 Davao, Phil.
53/K2 Davenport, Ia,US
58/E6 David, Pan.
43/F Davis (sea), Ant.
49/M3 Davis (str.), NAm.
52/B3 Davis, Ca,US
49/D3 Dawson, Can.
50/C2 Dawson Creek, BC,Can
28/F5 Daxian, China
54/C4 Dayton, Oh,US
57/H4 Daytona Beach, Fl,US
32/C2 Dead (sea), Asia
52/C3 Death Valley Nat'l Mon., Ca,Nv,US
21/J2 Debrecen, Hun.
57/G3 Decatur, Al,US
57/G3 Decatur, Ga,US
54/B4 Decatur, Il,US
34/C5 Deccan (plat.), India
54/C3 Defiance, Oh,US
33/L2 Dehra Dun, India
54/B3 De Kalb, Il,US
57/H4 De Land, Fl,US
54/F4 Delaware (bay), US
54/F3 Delaware (riv.), US
54/F4 Delaware (state), US
54/D3 Delaware, Oh,US
21/J4 Delfoi (ruins), Gre.
64/D5 Delgada (pt.), Arg.
34/C2 Delhi, India
21/F2 Dello Stelvio Nat'l Park, It.
57/H5 Delray Beach, Fl,US
56/C4 Del Rio, Tx,US
41/P5 Denakil (reg.), Erit., Eth.
18/F3 Den Helder, Neth.
23/C6 Denizli, Turk.
18/G3 Denmark
14/A2 Denmark (str.)
56/D3 Denton, Tx,US
53/F3 Denver (cap.), Co,US
33/J3 Dera Ghāzi Khān, Pak.
23/G5 Derbent, Rus.
18/D3 Derby, Eng,UK
18/B3 Derg, Lough (lake), Ire.
56/E4 De Ridder, La,US
55/G3 Derry, NH,US
64/C6 Deseado (riv.), Arg.
53/J2 Des Moines (cap.), Ia,US
23/D3 Desna (riv.), Eur.
64/A7 Desolación (isl.), Chile
18/H4 Dessau, Ger.
54/D3 Detroit, Mi,US
63/H2 Devil's (isl.), FrG.
49/J2 Devon (isl.), Can.
32/E2 Dezfūl, Iran
25/T3 Dezhnaya (cape), Rus.
28/H4 Dezhou, China
32/E3 Dhahran, SAr.
34/E3 Dhaka (Dacca) (cap.), Bang.
34/E3 Dhānbād, India
32/F5 Dhofar (reg.), Oman
34/B3 Dhulia, India
63/K6 Diamantina (uplands), Braz.
51/H4 Dickinson, ND,US
27/G10 Diego Garcia (isls.), BrIn.
35/H3 Dien Bien Phu, Viet.
20/D1 Dieppe, Fr.
37/J5 Digul (riv.), Indo.
20/E2 Dijon, Fr.
37/G5 Dili, Indo.
25/P2 Dimitriya Lapteva (str.), Rus.
21/H2 Dinaric Alps (mts.), Eur.
41/N5 Dinder Nat'l Park, Sudan
18/B3 Dingle (bay), Ire.
52/E2 Dinosaur Nat'l Mon., Co,Ut,US
41/P6 Dire Dawa, Eth.
63/J8 Divinópolis, Braz.
62/D5 Divisor (mts.), Braz.
54/B3 Dixon, Il,US
23/F6 Diyarbakir, Turk.
40/H3 Djado (plat.), Niger
36/C5 Djakarta (Jakarta), Indo.
41/P5 Djibouti
41/P5 Djibouti (cap.), Djib.
36/D5 Djokjakarta (Yogyakarta), Indo.
23/D4 Dnepr (Dnieper) (riv.), Eur.
23/D4 Dneprodzerzhinsk, Ukr.
23/D4 Dnepropetrovsk, Ukr.
23/C4 Dnestr (Dniester) (riv.), Eur.
37/H4 Doberai (pen.), Indo.
63/K7 Doce (riv.), Braz.
23/C6 Dodecanese (isls.), Gre.
53/G3 Dodge City, Ks,US
23/E5 Dogukaradeniz (mts.), Turk.
32/F3 Doha (cap.), Qatar
63/K5 Dois Irmãos (mts.), Braz.
64/C1 Domeyko (mts.), Chile
59/J4 Dominica
59/H4 Dominican Republic
23/F4 Don (riv.), Rus.
34/D6 Dondra (head), SrL.
18/B3 Donegal (bay), Ire.
23/E4 Donets (riv.), Ukr.
23/E4 Donetsk, Ukr.
30/B3 Dongguan, China
29/H4 Dongying, China
21/D2 Dordogne (riv.), Fr.
18/F4 Dortmund, Ger.
57/G4 Dothan, Al,US
40/G7 Douala, Camr.
18/C3 Douglas (cap.), IM,UK
52/E5 Douglas, Az,US
20/B3 Douro (riv.), Port.
18/E4 Dover (str.), Eur.
18/E4 Dover, Eng,UK
54/F4 Dover (cap.), De,US
55/G3 Dover, NH,US
64/C8 Drake (passage)
42/E6 Drakensburg (range), SAfr.
21/H2 Dráva (riv.), Eur.
19/H4 Dresden, Ger.
21/H2 Drina (riv.), Bosn.
45/D3 Drummond (range), Austl.
33/G3 Dubayyi (Dubai), UAE
18/C3 Dublin (cap.), Ire.
57/H3 Dublin, Ga,US
21/H3 Dubrovnik, Cro.
53/K2 Dubuque, Ia,US
24/J3 Dudinka, Rus.
20/E2 Dufourspitze (mt.), Eur.
62/E3 Duida Marahuaca Nat'l Park, Ven.
18/F4 Duisburg, Ger.
51/L4 Duluth, Mn,US
18/D3 Dumfries, Sc,UK
53/H4 Duncan, Ok,US
18/C3 Dundalk, Ire.
18/D2 Dundee, Sc,UK
45/H7 Dunedin, NZ
57/H4 Dunedin, Fl,US
20/D1 Dunkirk (Dunkerque), Fr.
59/P9 Durango, Mex.
52/F3 Durango, Co,US
53/H4 Durant, Ok,US
42/F6 Durban, SAfr.
34/E3 Durgapur, India
18/D3 Durham, Eng,UK
57/J3 Durham, NC,US
55/G3 Durham, NH,US
21/H3 Durrës, Alb.
24/G6 Dushanbe (cap.), Taj.
18/F4 Düsseldorf, Ger.
17/J2 Dvina, Northern (Dvina Severnaya) (riv.), Rus.
23/C2 Dvina, Western (Dvina Zapadnaya) (riv.), Bela.
23/F2 Dzerzhinsk, Rus.
31/B3 Dzhambul, Kaz.
24/G5 Dzhezkagan, Kaz.
25/P4 Dzhugdzhur (range), Rus.

E

56/C4 Eagle Pass, Tx,US
27/M6 East China (sea), Asia
47/Q7 Easter (isl.), Chile
34/C5 Eastern Ghats (mts.), India
64/E7 East Falkland (isl.), Falk.
18/F3 East Frisian (isls.), Ger.
54/C3 East Lansing, Mi,US
54/D3 East Liverpool, Oh,US
42/E7 East London, SAfr.
57/G3 East Point, Ga,US
25/S2 East Siberian (sea), Rus.
54/B4 East St. Louis, Il,US
54/B2 Eau Claire, Wi,US
20/D3 Ebro (riv.), Sp.
58/B4 Ecatepec, Mex.
20/E2 Écrins Nat'l Park, Fr.
62/C4 Ecuador
57/J2 Eden, NC,US
57/J2 Edenton, NC,US
56/D5 Edinburg, Tx,US
18/D3 Edinburgh (cap.), Sc,UK
23/C5 Edirne, Turk.
50/C4 Edmonds, Wa,US
50/E2 Edmonton (cap.), Ab,Can
55/G2 Edmundston, NB,Can
23/C6 Edremit, Turk.
56/C4 Edwards (plat.), Tx,US
54/B4 Edwardsville, Il,US
52/B3 Eel (riv.), Ca,US
54/B4 Effingham, Il,US
21/G4 Egadi (isls.), It.
45/H6 Egmont (mt.), NZ
41/L2 Egypt
18/F4 Eifel (plat.), Ger.
18/F4 Eindhoven, Neth.
40/F1 El Asnam, Alg.
32/B3 Elat (Elath), Isr.
23/E6 Elazig, Turk.
21/F3 Elba (isl.), It.
18/G3 Elbe (riv.), Ger.
52/F3 Elbert (mt.), Co,US
19/J3 Elblag, Pol.
23/F5 El'brus (mt.), Rus.
32/E1 Elburz (mts.), Iran
52/C4 El Cajon, Ca,US
52/D4 El Centro, Ca,US
62/D2 El Cocuy Nat'l Park, Col.
40/D3 El Djouf (des.), Mrta.
53/J4 El Dorado, Ar,US
17/H3 Elektrostal', Rus.
59/F2 Eleuthera (isl.), Bahm.
54/B3 Elgin, Il,US
41/M7 Elgon (mt.), Ugan.
57/J2 Elizabeth City, NC,US
54/C3 Elkhart, In,US
40/C3 El Khatt (escarp.), Mrta.
50/C4 Ellensburg, Wa,US
49/J2 Ellesmere (isl.), Can.
43/U Ellsworth Land (reg.), Ant.
54/E3 Elmira, NY,US
62/D7 El Misti (vol.), Peru
64/C4 El Nevado (mtn.), Arg.
56/A4 El Paso, Tx,US
52/H4 El Reno, Ok,US
58/D5 El Salvador
62/E2 El Tuparro Nat'l Park, Col.
62/D2 El Viejo (mtn.), Col.
54/D3 Elyria, Oh,US
63/H7 Emas Nat'l Park, Braz.
18/F3 Emden, Ger.
18/F3 Emmen, Neth.
53/H3 Emporia, Ks,US
18/F3 Ems (riv.), Eur.
43/D Enderby Land (reg.), Ant.
54/E3 Endicott, NY,US
46/F3 Enewetak (atoll), Mrsh.
23/G3 Engel's, Rus.
18/D3 England, UK
18/C4 English (chan.), Eur.
53/H3 Enid, Ok,US
41/K4 Ennedi (plat.), Chad
18/C3 Enniskillen, NI,UK
18/F3 Enschede, Neth.
59/L7 Ensenada, Mex.
41/M8 Entebbe, Ugan.
40/G6 Enugu, Nga.
32/E1 Enzeli (Bandar-e Anzali), Iran
20/E1 Épinal, Fr.
40/G7 Equatorial Guinea
28/E2 Erdenet, Mong.
63/G4 Erepecu (lake), Braz.
18/G4 Erfurt, Ger.
40/D3 Erg Chech (des.), Alg., Mali
40/D2 Erg Iguidi (des.), Alg., Mrta.
54/D3 Erie (lake), NAm.
54/D3 Erie, Pa,US
32/C5 Eritrea
18/G4 Erlangen, Ger.
34/C5 Erode, India
18/B3 Erris Head (pt.), Ire.
19/H4 Erzgebirge (mts.), Eur.
23/F6 Erzurum, Turk.
22/H3 Esbo (Espoo), Fin.
54/C2 Escanaba, Mi,US
52/C4 Escondido, Ca,US
32/F2 Esfahān, Iran
23/D6 Eskişehir, Turk.
62/C3 Esmeraldas, Ecu.
63/K7 Espinhaço (mts.), Braz.
46/F6 Espiritu Santo (isl.), Van.
22/H3 Espoo (Esbo), Fin.
18/F4 Essen, Ger.
62/G2 Essequibo (riv.), Guy.
64/D7 Estados (isl.), Arg.
19/L2 Estonia
20/A3 Estrella (mts.), Port.
63/J5 Estrondo (mts.), Braz.
41/N5 Ethiopia
41/N6 Ethiopian (plat.), Eth.
21/G4 Etna (vol.), It.
42/C4 Etosha Nat'l Park, Namb.
21/K4 Euboea (Évvoia) (isl.), Gre.
54/D3 Euclid, Oh,US
50/C4 Eugene, Or,US
56/E4 Eunice, La,US
27/D6 Euphrates (riv.), Asia
52/A2 Eureka, Ca,US
17/ Europe
53/F3 Evans (mt.), Co,US
54/C3 Evanston, Il,US
54/C4 Evansville, In,US
34/E2 Everest (mt.), Asia
50/C3 Everett, Wa,US
57/H5 Everglades Nat'l Pk., Fl,US
20/B4 Évora, Port.
21/K4 Évvoia (isl.), Gre.
18/C4 Exeter, Eng,UK
55/G3 Exeter, NH,US
18/D4 Exmoor Nat'l Park, Eng,UK
45/C4 Eyre (lake), Austl.
45/C4 Eyre (pen.), Austl.

F

49/C3 Fairbanks, Ak,US
54/C4 Fairfield, Oh,US
50/D4 Fairmont, WV,US
33/K2 Faisalabad, Pak.
56/D5 Falcon (res.), NAm.
18/C3 Falkirk, Sc,UK
64/D7 Falkland Islands, UK
55/G3 Fall River, Ma,US
18/C4 Falmouth, Eng,UK
32/B1 Famagusta, Cyp.
42/K11 Fandriana, Madg.
47/K4 Fanning (Tabuaeran) (isl.), Kiri.
52/B3 Farallon (isls.), Ca,US
51/J4 Fargo, ND,US
51/K5 Faribault, Mn,US
34/C2 Farīdābād, India
52/E3 Farmington, NM,US
20/B4 Faro, Port.
17/D2 Faroe (isls.), Den.
53/J3 Fayetteville, Ar,US
57/J3 Fayetteville, NC,US
18/G3 Fehmarn (isl.), Ger.
29/J3 Fengcheng, China
31/B3 Fergana, Uzb.
51/K4 Fergus Falls, Mn,US
21/F2 Ferrara, It.
64/C3 Fertil (val.), Arg.
40/E1 Fès, Mor.
40/H2 Fezzan (reg.), Libya
42/K11 Fianarantsoa, Madg.
63/L6 Fiera de Santana, Braz.
46/G6 Fiji
21/K3 Filippoi (ruins), Gre.
54/D3 Findlay, Oh,US
20/A3 Finisterre (cape), Sp.
22/H2 Finland
22/H4 Finland (gulf), Eur.
21/F3 Firenze (Florence), It.
33/K2 Firozpur, India
21/G2 Fiume (Rijeka), Cro.
52/E4 Flagstaff, Az,US
52/E2 Flaming Gorge (res.), US
50/B3 Flattery (cape), Wa,US
18/G3 Flensburg, Ger.
45/D4 Flinders (isl.), Austl.
45/C4 Flinders (ranges), Austl.
54/D3 Flint, Mi,US
57/G3 Florence, Al,US
57/J3 Florence, SC,US
21/F3 Florence (Firenze), It.
37/F5 Flores (isl.), Indo.
37/E5 Flores (sea), Indo.
64/G2 Florianópolis, Braz.
58/E3 Florida (str.), Cuba, Fl,US
57/H4 Florida (state), US
57/H5 Florida (bay), Fl,US
53/K3 Florissant, Mo,US
21/G3 Foggia, It.
54/B3 Fond du Lac, Wi,US
46/G5 Fongafale (cap.), Tuv.
58/D5 Fonseca (gulf), NAm.
20/D1 Fontainebleau, Fr.
30/C2 Foochow (Fuzhou), China
21/G2 Forli, It.
63/G6 Formosa (mts.), Braz.
63/L4 Fortaleza, Braz.
52/F2 Ft. Collins, Co,US
59/J5 Ft.-de-France (cap.), Mart.
53/J2 Ft. Dodge, Ia,US
18/D2 Forth (firth), Sc,UK
18/D2 Forth, Firth of (inlet), Sc,UK
57/H5 Ft. Lauderdale, Fl,US
50/E3 Ft. Macleod, Ab,Can
53/K2 Ft. Madison, Ia,US
49/F4 Ft. McMurray, Can
57/H5 Ft. Myers, Fl,US
50/G4 Ft. Peck Lake (res.), Mt,US
57/H5 Ft. Pierce, Fl,US
49/F4 Ft. Smith, NW,Can
53/J4 Ft. Smith, Ar,US
57/G4 Ft. Walton Beach, Fl,US
54/C3 Ft. Wayne, In,US
18/C2 Fort William, Sc,UK
56/D3 Ft. Worth, Tx,US
30/B3 Foshan, China
54/D3 Fostoria, Oh,US
40/C5 Fouta Djallon (reg.), Gui.
45/G7 Foveaux (str.), NZ
49/J3 Foxe (basin), Can
62/E7 Frailes (mts.), Bol.
63/J8 França, Braz.
20/D2 France
51/J5 Francis Case (lake), SD,US
42/E5 Francistown, Bots.
54/C3 Frankfort, In,US
54/C4 Frankfort (cap.), Ky,US
18/G4 Frankfurt am Main, Ger.
19/H3 Frankfurt an der Oder, Ger.
50/D3 Franklin D. Roosevelt (lake), Wa,US
24/F2 Franz Josef Land (isls.), Rus.
50/C3 Fraser (riv.), BC,Can
22/D5 Fredericia, Den.
54/E4 Frederick, Md,US
54/E4 Fredericksburg, Va,US
55/H2 Fredericton (cap.), NB,Can
22/D4 Frederikshavn, Den.
59/F2 Freeport, Bah.
54/B3 Freeport, Il,US
40/C6 Freetown (cap.), SLeo.
18/F5 Freiburg, Ger.
50/B3 Fremont, Ca,US
53/H2 Fremont, Ne,US
63/H3 French Guiana
47/M6 French Polynesia
52/C3 Fresno, Ca,US
20/E2 Fribourg, Swi.
45/D4 Frome (lake), Austl.
52/F3 Front (range), Co,US
57/J2 Front Royal, Va,US
31/B3 Frunze (Bishkek) (cap.), Kyr.
29/M4 Fukui, Japan
29/L5 Fukuoka, Japan
29/N4 Fukushima, Japan
33/J2 Fūlādī (mtn.), Afg.
53/K3 Fulton, Mo,US
40/B1 Funchal, Port.
55/H2 Fundy (bay), NAm.
55/H2 Fundy Nat'l Pk., NB,Can
63/J8 Furnas (res.), Braz.

68

Furne – Kiev

45/D4 **Furneaux Group** (isls.), Austl.
18/G4 **Fürth,** Ger.
29/J3 **Fushun,** China
29/J3 **Fuxin,** China
30/C2 **Fuzhou,** China

G

40/H7 **Gabon**
42/E5 **Gaborone** (cap.), Bots.
57/G3 **Gadsden,** Al,US
21/G3 **Gaeta** (gulf), It.
57/H3 **Gaffney,** SC,US
57/H4 **Gainesville,** Fl,US
57/H3 **Gainesville,** Ga,US
45/C4 **Gairdner** (lake), Austl.
14/E6 **Galápagos** (isls.), Ecu.
21/K2 **Galaţi,** Rom.
54/B3 **Galesburg,** Il,US
57/G2 **Gallatin,** Tn,US
34/D6 **Galle,** SrL.
64/B7 **Gallegos** (riv.), Arg.
62/D1 **Gallinas** (pt.), Col.
23/C5 **Gallipoli,** Turk.
52/E4 **Gallup,** NM,US
52/E4 **Galveston,** Tx,US
18/B3 **Galway,** Ire.
41/M6 **Gambela Nat'l Park,** Eth.
40/B5 **Gambia**
40/B5 **Gambia** (riv.), Gam., Sen.
47/M7 **Gambier** (isls.), FrPol.
55/L1 **Gander,** Nf,Can
34/B3 **Gandhinagar,** India
31/D5 **Gangdise** (mts.), China
27/H7 **Ganges** (riv.), Asia
34/E3 **Ganges, Mouths of the** (delta), Bang., India
34/E2 **Gangtok,** India
30/C2 **Ganzhou,** China
20/E2 **Gap,** Fr.
41/L7 **Garamba Nat'l Park,** Zaire
21/F2 **Garda** (lake), It.
53/G3 **Garden City,** Ks,US
52/D3 **Garland,** Tx,US
21/F2 **Garmisch-Partenkirchen,** Ger.
20/D2 **Garonne** (riv.), Fr.
54/C3 **Gary,** In,US
36/C4 **Gaspar** (str.), Indo.
55/H1 **Gaspé** (pen.), Qu,Can
57/H3 **Gastonia,** NC,US
35/F2 **Gauhāti,** India
45/C4 **Gawler** (range), Austl.
34/E3 **Gaya,** India
32/B2 **Gaza,** Gaza
32/B2 **Gaza Strip**
23/E6 **Gaziantep,** Turk.
19/J3 **Gdańsk,** Pol.
19/J3 **Gdańsk** (gulf), Pol.
19/J3 **Gdynia,** Pol.
45/D4 **Geelong,** Austl.
35/H3 **Gejiu,** China
42/D6 **Gemsbok Nat'l Park,** Bots.
64/B6 **General Carrera** (lake), Chile
20/E2 **Geneva,** Swi.
54/E3 **Geneva,** NY,US
20/E2 **Geneva** (Léman) (lake), Eur.
21/F2 **Genoa** (Genova), It.
21/F2 **Genova** (gulf), It.
58/E4 **George Town** (cap.), Cay.
62/G2 **Georgetown** (cap.), Guy.
36/B2 **George Town** (Pinang), Malay.
23/F5 **Georgia**
50/C3 **Georgia** (str.), BC,Can
57/G3 **Georgia** (state), US
54/D2 **Georgian** (bay), On,Can
18/H4 **Gera,** Ger.
63/J6 **Geral de Goias** (mts.), Braz.
18/G4 **Germany**
54/E4 **Gettysburg,** Pa,US
40/E6 **Ghana**
34/C2 **Ghaziābād,** India
33/J2 **Ghazni,** Afg.
18/E4 **Ghent,** Belg.
20/B5 **Gibraltar** (str.)
20/B4 **Gibraltar,** UK
45/B3 **Gibson** (des.), Austl.
29/M4 **Gifu,** Japan
20/B3 **Gijón,** Sp.
52/D4 **Gila** (riv.), US
46/G5 **Gilbert Is.** (Kiribati)
50/G4 **Gillette,** Wy,US
20/D3 **Girona** (Gerona), Sp.
20/C2 **Gironde** (riv.), Fr.
25/R3 **Gizhiga** (bay), Rus.
55/K2 **Glace Bay,** NS,Can
64/B6 **Glaciares Nat'l Park,** Arg.
50/D2 **Glacier Nat'l Pk.,** BC,Can
50/E3 **Glacier Nat'l Pk.,** Mt,US
18/C3 **Glasgow,** Sc,UK
52/D4 **Glendale,** Az,US
52/C4 **Glendale,** Ca,US
55/F3 **Glens Falls,** NY,US
18/D4 **Gloucester,** Eng,UK
34/B4 **Goa** (dist.), India
63/J7 **Goânia,** Braz.
28/E3 **Gobi** (des.), Asia
34/D4 **Godavari** (riv.), India
64/C3 **Godoy Cruz,** Arg.
49/M3 **Godthåb** (Nuuk) (cap.), Grld.
33/L1 **Godwin Austen** (K2) (mt.), Asia
63/J7 **Goiânia,** Braz.
45/E3 **Gold Coast,** Austl.
40/E7 **Gold Coast** (reg.), Gha.
53/F3 **Golden,** Co,US
57/J3 **Goldsboro,** NC,US
19/M3 **Gomel',** Bela.
59/G4 **Gonâve** (gulf), Haiti
41/N5 **Gonder,** Eth.
42/C7 **Good Hope** (cape), SAfr.
52/B2 **Goose** (lake), US
49/L4 **Goose Bay-Happy Valley,** Nf,Can
34/D2 **Gorakhpur,** India
33/F2 **Gorgān,** Iran
23/F2 **Gor'kiy** (res.), Rus.
23/F2 **Gor'kiy** (Nizhniy Novgorod), Rus.
23/E4 **Gorlovka,** Ukr.
37/F3 **Gorontalo,** Indo.
23/C4 **Gorya** (riv.), Ukr.
19/H4 **Gorzow Wielkopolski,** Pol.
21/J3 **Gostivar,** Macd.
22/D4 **Göteborg,** Swe.
22/F4 **Gotland** (isl.), Swe.
18/G4 **Göttingen,** Ger.
19/L4 **Goverla, Gora** (mt.), Ukr.
63/K7 **Governador Baladares,** Braz.
28/D3 **Govi Altayn** (mts.), Mong.
24/G1 **Graham Bell** (isl.), Rus.
40/D6 **Grain Coast** (reg.), Libr.
18/C2 **Grampian** (mts.), Sc,UK
20/C4 **Granada,** Sp.
64/C6 **Gran Altiplanicie Central** (plat.), Arg.
64/C6 **Gran Bajo Oriental** (val.), Arg.
40/B2 **Gran Canaria** (isl.), Sp.
64/D2 **Gran Chaco** (reg.), SAm.
59/F2 **Grand Bahama** (isl.), Bahm.
52/D3 **Grand Canyon Nat'l Pk.,** Az,US
58/E4 **Grand Cayman** (isl.), Cay.
62/F7 **Grande** (riv.), Bol.
63/J7 **Grande** (riv.), Braz.
63/K6 **Grande** (riv.), Braz.
50/D2 **Grande Prairie,** Ab,Can
40/H4 **Grand 'Erg de Bilma** (des.), Niger
40/E1 **Grand Erg Occidental** (des.), Alg.
40/G1 **Grand Erg Oriental** (des.), Alg., Tun.
56/C4 **Grande, Rio** (riv.), NAm.
59/J4 **Grande-Terre** (isl.), Guad.
51/J4 **Grand Forks,** ND,US
53/H2 **Grand Island,** Ne,US
52/E3 **Grand Junction,** Co,US
55/H2 **Grand Manan** (isl.), NB,Can
54/C3 **Grand Rapids,** Mi,US
50/F5 **Grand Teton Nat'l Pk.,** Wy,US
59/G3 **Grand Turk** (cap.), Trks.
57/F2 **Granite City,** Il,US
62/F2 **Gran Sabana, La** (plain), Ven.
52/F4 **Grants,** NM,US
50/C5 **Grants Pass,** Or,US
62/C5 **Gran Vilaya** (ruins), Peru
20/E3 **Grasse,** Fr.
21/G2 **Graz,** Aus.
59/F2 **Great Abaco** (isl.), Bahm.
45/B4 **Great Australian** (bight), Austl.
45/D2 **Great Barrier** (reef), Austl.
50/C2 **Great Basin** (basin), US
52/D3 **Great Basin Nat'l Park,** Nv,US
49/E3 **Great Bear** (lake), Can.
53/H3 **Great Bend,** Ks,US
18/D2 **Great Britain** (isl.), UK
45/D4 **Great Dividing** (range), Austl.
59/F3 **Greater Antilles** (isls.), NAm.
36/C4 **Greater Sunda** (isls.), Indo.
59/F3 **Great Exuma** (isl.), Bahm.
50/F4 **Great Falls,** Mt,US
59/G3 **Great Inagua** (isl.), Bahm.
34/B2 **Great Indian** (Thar) (des.), India
42/D7 **Great Karoo** (reg.), SAfr.
53/G2 **Great Plains** (plains), US
42/F2 **Great Rift** (val.), Afr.
41/N6 **Great Rift** (val.), Djib., Eth.
52/D2 **Great Salt** (lake), Ut,US
41/K2 **Great Sand Sea** (des.), Afr.
45/B2 **Great Sandy** (des.), Austl.
49/F3 **Great Slave** (lake), NW,Can
57/H3 **Great Smoky Mts. Nat'l Pk.,** NC,Tn,US
45/B3 **Great Victoria** (des.), Austl.
28/F4 **Great Wall,** China
21/J4 **Greece**
53/F2 **Greeley,** Co,US
52/E3 **Green** (riv.), US
55/F3 **Green** (mts.), Vt,US
54/B2 **Green Bay,** Wi,US
57/H2 **Greeneville,** Tn,US
55/F3 **Greenfield,** Ma,US
49/R2 **Greenland** (sea)
49/N2 **Greenland,** Den.
18/C3 **Greenock,** Sc,UK
57/J2 **Greensboro,** NC,US
54/E3 **Greensburg,** Pa,US
57/F3 **Greenville,** Ms,US
57/J3 **Greenville,** NC,US
57/H3 **Greenville,** SC,US
57/F3 **Greenwood,** Ms,US
57/H3 **Greenwood,** SC,US
45/D2 **Gregory** (range), Austl.
59/J5 **Grenada**
20/E2 **Grenoble,** Fr.
57/F4 **Gretna,** La,US
45/D3 **Grey** (range), Austl.
57/G3 **Griffin,** Ga,US
18/D3 **Grimsby,** Eng,UK
19/K3 **Grodno,** Bela.
18/F3 **Groningen,** Neth.
45/C2 **Groote Eylandt** (isl.), Austl.
21/G2 **Grossglockner** (mt.), Aus.
23/G5 **Groznyy,** Rus.
59/F3 **Guacanaybo** (gulf), Cuba
58/A3 **Guadalajara,** Mex.
20/C3 **Guadalajara,** Sp.
46/E6 **Guadalcanal** (isl.), Sol.
20/B4 **Guadalquivir** (riv.), Sp.
58/B2 **Guadalupe,** Mex.
56/B3 **Guadalupe** (mts.), US
56/B4 **Guadalupe Mts. Nat'l Pk.,** Tx,US
20/B3 **Guadarama** (mts.), Sp.
59/J4 **Guadeloupe,** Fr.
59/J4 **Guadeloupe Passage** (chan.), West Indies
20/B4 **Guadiana** (riv.), Eur.
64/B5 **Guafo** (str.), Chile
62/E3 **Guainiá** (riv.), Col.
62/D1 **Guajira** (pen.), SAm.
64/C5 **Gualicho** (marsh), Arg.
46/D3 **Guam**
28/F5 **Guangyuan,** China
30/B3 **Guangzhou** (Canton), China
59/F3 **Guantánamo,** Cuba
62/F6 **Guaporé** (Iténez) (riv.), Braz.
62/E2 **Guárico** (res.), Ven.
58/C4 **Guatemala**
58/C5 **Guatemala** (cap.), Guat.
62/E3 **Guaviare** (riv.), Col.
62/B4 **Guayaquil,** Ecu.
62/B4 **Guayaquil** (gulf), Ecu.
59/M8 **Guaymas,** Mex.
19/H3 **Guben** (Wilhelm-Pieck-Stadt), Ger.
54/D3 **Guelph,** On,Can
18/D4 **Guernsey** (isl.), Chl.
62/F2 **Guiana Highlands** (mts.), SAm.
30/B2 **Guilin,** China
40/C5 **Guinea**
40/F7 **Guinea** (gulf), Afr.
40/B5 **Guinea-Bissau**
35/J2 **Guiyang,** China
35/K2 **Gujranwala,** Pak.
33/K2 **Gujrāt,** Pak.
34/C4 **Gulbarga,** India
56/D5 **Gulf Coastal** (plain), Tx,US
57/F4 **Gulfport,** Ms,US
23/F6 **Güneydogu Toroslar** (mts.), Turk.
34/D4 **Guntur,** India
64/F2 **Gural** (mts.), Braz.
62/F2 **Guri** (res.), Ven.
63/H4 **Gurupá, Grande de** (isl.), Braz.
63/J4 **Gurupi** (mts.), Braz.
63/J4 **Gurupi** (riv.), Braz.
23/H4 **Gur'yev,** Kaz.
53/H4 **Guthrie,** Ok,US
62/G3 **Guyana**
34/C2 **Gwalior,** India
42/E4 **Gweru,** Zim.
23/G5 **Gyandzhe,** Azer.
24/H2 **Gyda** (pen.), Rus.
21/H2 **Győr,** Hun.

H

18/F3 **Haarlem,** Neth.
32/E5 **Hadhramaut** (reg.), Yem.
29/K4 **Haeju,** NKor.
54/E4 **Hagerstown,** Md,US
18/F3 **Hague, The** (cap.), Neth.
29/J3 **Haicheng,** China
32/B2 **Haifa,** Isr.
30/B3 **Haikou,** China
30/B4 **Hainan** (isl.), China
29/J5 **Haining,** China
35/J3 **Haiphong,** Viet.
59/G4 **Haiti**
29/N3 **Hakodate,** Japan
32/C1 **Halab** (Aleppo), Syria
45/D2 **Halifax** (bay), Austl.
55/J2 **Halifax** (cap.), NS,Can
18/G4 **Halle,** Ger.
37/G3 **Halmahera** (isl.), Indo.
37/G4 **Halmahera** (sea), Indo.
22/E4 **Hälsingborg,** Swe.
32/E2 **Hamadan,** Iran
32/C1 **Hamāh,** Syria
29/M5 **Hamamatsu,** Japan
18/G3 **Hamburg,** Ger.
45/A3 **Hamersley** (range), Austl.
29/K3 **Hamgyong** (mts.), NKor.
29/K3 **Hamhung,** NKor.
54/E3 **Hamilton,** On,Can
45/H6 **Hamilton,** NZ
54/C4 **Hamilton,** Oh,US
18/F3 **Hamm,** Ger.
22/G1 **Hammerfest,** Nor.
54/C3 **Hammond,** In,US
57/F4 **Hammond,** La,US
54/E4 **Hampton,** Va,US
40/H3 **Hamrā, Al Hamādah al** (upland), Libya
29/K4 **Han** (riv.), SKor.
28/G4 **Handan,** China
52/C3 **Hanford,** Ca,US
28/D2 **Hangayn** (mts.), Mong.
30/D1 **Hangzhou** (Hangchow), China
53/K3 **Hannibal,** Mo,US
18/G3 **Hannover,** Ger.
35/J3 **Hanoi** (cap.), Viet.
55/F3 **Hanover,** NH,US
28/F5 **Hanzhong,** China
42/F4 **Harare** (cap.), Zim.
29/K2 **Harbin,** China
41/P6 **Hargeysa,** Som.
56/D5 **Harlingen,** Tx,US
54/E3 **Harrisburg** (cap.), Pa,US
54/E4 **Harrisonburg,** Va,US
54/C4 **Harrodsburg,** Ky,US
55/F3 **Hartford** (cap.), Ct,US
18/D3 **Hartlepool,** Eng,UK
18/G4 **Harz** (mts.), Ger.
53/H2 **Hastings,** Ne,US
57/F4 **Hattiesburg,** Ms,US
41/Q6 **Haud** (reg.), Eth.
58/E3 **Havana** (cap.), Cuba
52/D4 **Havasu** (lake), US
55/G3 **Haverhill,** Ma,US
50/F3 **Havre,** Mt,US
47/K2 **Hawaii** (state), US
47/K3 **Hawaii** (isl.), Hi,US
47/H2 **Hawaiian** (isls.), US
32/E3 **Ḩawalli,** Kuw.
49/F3 **Hay River,** NW,Can
53/H3 **Hays,** Ks,US
50/A2 **Hazleton** (mts.), BC,Can
54/F3 **Hazleton,** Pa,US
28/G4 **Hebi,** China
18/C2 **Hebrides, Inner** (isls.), Sc,UK
18/B2 **Hebrides, Outer** (isls.), Sc,UK
29/H5 **Hefei,** China
29/L2 **Hegang,** China
18/G4 **Heidelberg,** Ger.
18/G4 **Heilbronn,** Ger.
29/J1 **Heilong** (riv.), China
22/N7 **Hekla** (mt.), Ice.
28/F4 **Helan** (mts.), China
50/F4 **Helena** (cap.), Mt,US
33/H2 **Helmand** (riv.), Afg.
22/H3 **Helsinki** (cap.), Fin.
57/G2 **Henderson,** Ky,US
57/J2 **Henderson,** NC,US
52/D3 **Henderson,** Nv,US
35/G2 **Hengduan** (mts.), China
30/B2 **Hengyang,** China
33/H2 **Herat,** Afg.
59/M8 **Hermosillo,** Mex.
57/H5 **Hialeah,** Fl,US
51/K4 **Hibbing,** Mn,US
57/H3 **Hickory,** NC,US
57/H3 **High Point,** NC,US
19/K2 **Hiiumaa** (isl.), Est.
32/C3 **Hijāz, Jabal al** (mts.), SAr.
50/C4 **Hillsboro,** Or,US
47/K3 **Hilo,** Hi,US
27/G6 **Himalaya** (mts.), Asia
32/C2 **Ḩimş,** Syria
33/J1 **Hindu Kush** (mts.), Asia
29/N3 **Hirosaki,** Japan
29/L5 **Hiroshima,** Japan
59/G4 **Hispaniola** (isl.), NAm.
29/N4 **Hitachi,** Japan
45/D5 **Hobart,** Austl.
53/G4 **Hobbs,** NM,US
35/J5 **Ho Chi Minh City** (Saigon), Viet.
21/F2 **Hohe Tauern** (range), Aus.
28/G3 **Hohhot,** China
29/N3 **Hokkaidō** (isl.), Japan
59/F3 **Holguin,** Cuba
54/C3 **Holland,** Mi,US
57/H5 **Hollywood,** Fl,US
18/C3 **Holyhead,** Wal,UK
55/F3 **Holyoke,** Ma,US
57/H5 **Homestead,** Fl,US
58/D4 **Honduras**
58/D4 **Honduras** (gulf), NAm.
30/B3 **Hong Kong,** UK
46/E5 **Honiara** (cap.), Sol.
47/K2 **Honolulu** (cap.), Hi,US
29/M5 **Honshu** (isl.), Japan
50/C4 **Hood** (mt.), Or,US
52/D3 **Hoover** (dam), US
56/E3 **Hope,** Ar,US
54/E4 **Hopewell,** Va,US
54/B4 **Hopkinsville,** Ky,US
33/G3 **Hormuz** (str.), Asia
64/C8 **Horn** (cape), Chile
54/E3 **Hornell,** NY,US
21/J2 **Hortobágyi Nat'l Park,** Hun.
56/E3 **Hot Springs Nat'l Park,** Ar,US
57/F4 **Houma,** La,US
56/E4 **Houston,** Tx,US
28/E1 **Hövsgöl** (lake), Mong.
47/H4 **Howland** (isl.), PacUS
34/E3 **Howrah,** India
19/H4 **Hradec Králové,** Czh.
30/D3 **Hsinchu,** Tai.
28/H5 **Huaibei,** China
30/B2 **Huaihua,** China
29/H5 **Huainan,** China
42/C3 **Huambo,** Ang.
62/C6 **Huancayo,** Peru
62/E8 **Huanchaca** (peak), Bol.
29/H4 **Huang He** (Yellow) (riv.), China
30/C2 **Huangshi,** China
62/C5 **Huascarán** (mt.), Peru
62/C5 **Huascarán Nat'l Park,** Peru
62/E6 **Huatunas** (lake), Bol.
28/F5 **Huaying,** China
34/C4 **Hubli-Dharwar,** India
18/D3 **Huddersfield,** Eng,UK
49/J3 **Hudson** (bay), Can.
49/K3 **Hudson** (str.), Can.
54/F3 **Hudson** (riv.), US
35/J4 **Hue,** Viet.
20/B4 **Huelva,** Sp.
42/B4 **Huila** (plat.), Ang.
62/C3 **Huila** (peak), Col.
54/F2 **Hull,** Qu,Can
18/D3 **Hull,** Eng,UK
28/H2 **Hulun** (lake), China
52/E4 **Humphreys** (peak), Az,US
21/H2 **Hungary**
29/K4 **Hŭngnam,** NKor.
29/K3 **Hunjiang,** China
54/C3 **Huntington,** In,US
54/D4 **Huntington,** WV,US
52/C4 **Huntington Beach,** Ca,US
57/G3 **Huntsville,** Al,US
56/E4 **Huntsville,** Tx,US
54/D2 **Huron** (lake), NAm.
51/J4 **Huron,** SD,US
53/H3 **Hutchinson,** Ks,US
29/J5 **Huzhou,** China
42/E4 **Hwange Nat'l Park,** Zim.
34/C4 **Hyderabad,** India
33/J3 **Hyderabad,** Pak.
20/E3 **Hyères** (isls.), Fr.

I

21/K2 **Iaşi,** Rom.
40/F6 **Ibadan,** Nga.
62/C3 **Ibagué,** Col.
64/E2 **Iberá** (marsh), Arg.
20/C3 **Iberica, Sistema** (range), Sp.
20/D4 **Ibiza** (isl.), Sp.
62/E4 **Iça** (riv.), Braz.
22/N7 **Iceland**
28/G5 **Ichang** (Yichang), China
50/E5 **Idaho** (state), US
50/E5 **Idaho Falls,** Id,US
40/F6 **Ife,** Nga.
40/F3 **Iforas, Ardar des** (mts.), Alg., Mali
64/F2 **Iguaçu** (riv.), Braz.
64/F2 **Iguazú** (falls), SAm.
64/F2 **Iguazu Nat'l Park,** Arg.
40/D2 **Iguidi, Èrg** (des.), Alg.
21/K4 **Ikaria** (isl.), Gre.
47/X15 **Iles du Vent** (isls.), FrPol.
40/F6 **Ilesha,** Nga.
63/H7 **Ilha Salteira** (res.), Braz.
62/E7 **Illimani** (mtn.), Bol.
54/B4 **Illinois** (state), US
54/B3 **Illinois** (riv.), Il,US
23/D2 **Il'men** (lake), Rus.
30/D5 **Iloilo,** Phil.
40/F6 **Ilorin,** Nga.
63/J5 **Imperatriz,** Braz.
35/F3 **Imphal,** India
29/K4 **Inch'ŏn,** SKor.
53/J3 **Independence,** Ks,US
53/J3 **Independence,** Mo,US
27/G7 **India**
54/C3 **Indiana** (state), US
54/E3 **Indiana,** Pa,US
54/C4 **Indianapolis** (cap.), In,US
15/N6 **Indian Ocean**
25/Q3 **Indigirka** (riv.), Rus.
52/C4 **Indio,** Ca,US
35/C1 **Indochina** (reg.), Asia
36/E4 **Indonesia**
34/C3 **Indore,** India
27/F7 **Indus** (riv.), Asia
62/C4 **Ingapirca** (ruins), Ecu.
18/G4 **Ingolstadt,** Ger.
21/G1 **Inn** (riv.), Eur.
18/C2 **Inner Hebrides** (isls.), Sc,UK
28/G3 **Inner Mongolia** (reg.), China
21/F2 **Innsbruck,** Aus.
35/G4 **Insein,** Burma
50/B2 **Interior** (plat.), BC,Can
51/H3 **International Peace Garden,** NAm.
49/D3 **Inuvik,** Can.
45/G6 **Invercargill,** NZ
18/C2 **Inverness,** Sc,UK
42/B4 **Iona Nat'l Park,** Ang.
21/H4 **Ionian** (sea), Eur.
21/H4 **Ionian** (isls.), Gre.
53/J2 **Iowa** (state), US
53/K2 **Iowa City,** Ia,US
63/K7 **Ipatinga,** Braz.
36/B3 **Ipoh,** Malay.
18/E3 **Ipswich,** Eng,UK
49/L3 **Iqualuit,** Can.
62/D8 **Iquique,** Chile
62/D4 **Iquitos,** Peru
21/K5 **Iráklion,** Gre.
27/E6 **Iran**
58/A3 **Irapuato,** Mex.
32/D2 **Iraq**
32/D1 **Irbil,** Iraq
18/B3 **Ireland**
18/C3 **Ireland, Northern,** UK
37/J4 **Irian Jaya** (reg.), Indo.
63/H4 **Iriri** (riv.), Braz.
18/C3 **Irish** (sea), Eur.
28/E1 **Irkutsk,** Rus.
21/J2 **Iron Gate** (gorge), Rom.
54/D4 **Ironton,** Oh,US
35/G4 **Irrawaddy** (riv.), Burma
35/F4 **Irrawaddy, Mouths of the** (delta), Burma
24/G4 **Irtysh** (riv.), Rus.
52/C4 **Irvine,** Ca,US
53/H4 **Irving,** Tx,US
42/J11 **Isala Massif** (mts.), Madg.
18/G4 **Isar** (riv.), Ger.
20/E2 **Isère** (riv.), Fr.
40/F6 **Iseyin,** Nga.
62/E7 **Isiboro Securé Nat'l Park,** Bol.
23/E6 **Iskenderun,** Turk.
21/J3 **Iskŭr** (riv.), Bul.
33/K2 **Islamabad** (cap.), Pak.
64/B5 **Isla Magdalena Nat'l Park,** Chile
18/C3 **Isle of Man,** UK
54/B1 **Isle Royale** (isl.), Mi,US
54/B2 **Isle Royale Nat'l Pk.,** Mi,US
32/B2 **Ismailia,** Egypt
23/D6 **Isparta,** Turk.
32/B2 **Israel**
31/C3 **Issyk-Kul'** (lake), Kyr.
23/C5 **Istanbul,** Turk.
21/G2 **Istria** (pen.), Cro.
63/L6 **Itabuna,** Braz.
64/E1 **Itaipu** (res.), Braz., Par.
21/F3 **Italy**
63/K7 **Itambé** (peak), Braz.
63/L6 **Itapicuru** (riv.), Braz.
62/F6 **Iténez** (Guaporé) (riv.), Bol.
54/E3 **Ithaca,** NY,US
23/B4 **Ivano-Frankovsk,** Ukr.
23/F2 **Ivanovo,** Rus.
40/D6 **Ivory Coast** (Côte d'Ivoire)
40/D7 **Ivory Coast** (reg.), IvC.
57/N4 **Iwaki,** Japan
46/D2 **Iwo Jima** (isl.), Japan
23/H2 **Izhevsk,** Rus.
33/G4 **Izkī,** Oman
23/C6 **Izmir,** Turk.
23/C5 **Izmit,** Turk.

J

34/C3 **Jabalpur,** India
54/C3 **Jackson,** Mi,US
57/F3 **Jackson** (cap.), Ms,US
57/F3 **Jackson,** Tn,US
56/E3 **Jacksonville,** Ar,US
57/H4 **Jacksonville,** Fl,US
54/B4 **Jacksonville,** Il,US
57/J3 **Jacksonville,** NC,US
20/C4 **Jaén,** Sp.
34/C6 **Jaffna,** SrL.
34/C2 **Jaipur,** India
36/C5 **Jakarta** (cap.), Indo.
33/K2 **Jalālābād,** Afg.
58/B4 **Jalapa,** Mex.
34/C3 **Jalgaon,** India
59/F4 **Jamaica**
59/F4 **Jamaica** (chan.), Haiti, Jam.
63/G5 **Jamanxim** (riv.), Braz.
36/B4 **Jambi,** Indo.
49/J4 **James** (bay), Can.
54/E4 **James** (riv.), Va,US
51/J4 **Jamestown,** ND,US
54/E3 **Jamestown,** NY,US
33/K2 **Jammu,** India
33/K2 **Jammu & Kashmir** (state), India
34/B3 **Jamnagar,** India
34/E3 **Jamshedpur,** India
63/J3 **Janaucu** (isl.), Braz.
54/B3 **Janesville,** Wi,US
17/D1 **Jan Mayen** (isl.), Nor.
29/M4 **Japan**
29/L3 **Japan** (sea), Asia
29/M4 **Japanese Alps** (mts.), Japan
62/E4 **Japurá** (riv.), Braz.
63/H3 **Jari** (riv.), Braz.
47/J5 **Jarvis** (isl.), Pacific
63/H4 **Jauaru** (mts.), Braz.
62/F3 **Jaua Sarisarinama Nat'l Park,** Ven.
36/C5 **Java** (isl.), Indo.
36/D5 **Java** (sea), Indo.
37/K4 **Jayapura,** Indo.
53/J3 **Jefferson City** (cap.), Mo,US
54/C4 **Jeffersonville,** In,US
36/D5 **Jember,** Indo.
18/G4 **Jena,** Ger.
63/K7 **Jequitinhonha** (riv.), Braz.
20/B4 **Jerez de la Frontera,** Sp.
18/D4 **Jersey** (isl.), Chl.
32/D2 **Jerusalem** (cap.), Isr.
55/N6 **Jésus** (isl.), Qu,Can
21/H3 **Jezerce** (mt.), Alb.
33/K2 **Jhang Sadar,** Pak.
34/C2 **Jhansi,** India
33/K2 **Jhelum,** Pak.
29/L2 **Jiamusi,** China
30/D2 **Jiaojiang,** China
28/G4 **Jiaozuo,** China
29/J5 **Jiaxing,** China
32/C4 **Jiddah,** SAr.
29/K3 **Jilin,** China
29/H4 **Jinan** (Tsinan), China
30/C2 **Jingdezhen,** China
28/G5 **Jingmen,** China
30/C2 **Jinhua,** China
28/G3 **Jining,** China
29/J3 **Jinzhou,** China
30/C2 **Jiujiang,** China
29/L2 **Jixi,** China
32/D5 **Jizān,** SAr.
63/M5 **João Pessoa,** Braz.
34/B2 **Jodhpur,** India
42/E6 **Johannesburg,** SAfr.
50/C4 **John Day** (riv.), Or,US
57/H2 **Johnson City,** Tn,US
47/J3 **Johnston** (atoll), PacUS
54/E3 **Johnstown,** Pa,US
36/B3 **Johor Baharu,** Malay.
64/G2 **Joinvile,** Braz.
54/B3 **Joliet,** Il,US
57/F3 **Jonesboro,** Ar,US
22/E4 **Jönköping,** Swe.
55/G1 **Jonquière,** Qu,Can
53/J3 **Joplin,** Mo,US
32/C2 **Jordan**
32/C2 **Jordan** (riv.), Asia
40/G6 **Jos** (plat.), Nga.
45/B2 **Joseph Bonaparte** (gulf), Austl.
50/B3 **Juan de Fuca** (str.), NAm.
61/A6 **Juan Fernández** (isls.), Chile
63/L5 **Juazeiro do Norte,** Braz.
20/C4 **Júcar** (riv.), Sp.
63/K8 **Juiz de Fora,** Braz.
63/G3 **Juliana Top** (peak), Sur.
33/L2 **Jullundur,** India
53/H3 **Junction City,** Ks,US
63/J8 **Jundiaí,** Braz.
49/D4 **Juneau** (cap.), Ak,US
20/F2 **Jungfrau** (mt.), Swi.
20/E2 **Jura** (mts.), Eur.
62/E4 **Juruá** (riv.), Braz.
58/E3 **Juventud** (isl.), Cuba

K

33/L1 **K2** (mt.), Asia
41/M7 **Kabalega Nat'l Park,** Ugan.
33/J2 **Kabul** (cap.), Afg.
42/E3 **Kabwe,** Zam.
40/G5 **Kaduna,** Nga.
29/K4 **Kaesŏng,** NKor.
42/E4 **Kafue** (riv.), Zam.
42/E3 **Kafue Nat'l Park,** Zam.
29/L5 **Kagoshima,** Japan
23/E6 **Kahramanmaras,** Turk.
37/H5 **Kai** (isls.), Indo.
28/G5 **Kaifeng,** China
18/G4 **Kaiserslautern,** Ger.
35/H3 **Kaiyuan,** China
34/D4 **Kakinada,** India
49/N2 **Kalaallit Nunaat** (Greenland), Den.
42/D5 **Kalahari** (des.), Afr.
42/C6 **Kalahari-Gemsbok Nat'l Park,** Bots.
54/C3 **Kalamazoo,** Mi,US
41/K2 **Kalanshiyū, Sahīr** (des.), Libya
28/G3 **Kalgan** (Zhangjiakou), China
36/D4 **Kalimantan** (reg.), Indo.
19/K3 **Kaliningrad** (Königsberg), Rus.
19/J4 **Kalisz,** Pol.
23/E3 **Kaluga,** Rus.
25/R3 **Kalyma** (riv.), Rus.
17/K3 **Kama** (riv.), Rus.
25/R4 **Kamchatka** (pen.), Rus.
23/C4 **Kamenets-Podol'skiy,** Ukr.
24/G4 **Kamensk-Ural'skiy,** Rus.
50/C3 **Kamloops,** BC,Can
41/M7 **Kampala** (cap.), Ugan.
23/G3 **Kamyshin,** Rus.
42/D2 **Kananga,** Zaire
29/M4 **Kanazawa,** Japan
34/E2 **Kanchenjunga** (mt.), Asia
34/D6 **Kandy,** SrL.
45/C4 **Kangaroo** (isl.), Austl.
35/F2 **Kangto** (peak), China, India
24/E3 **Kanin** (pen.), Rus.
54/C3 **Kankakee,** Il,US
57/H3 **Kannapolis,** NC,US
41/G5 **Kano,** Nga.
34/D2 **Kānpur,** India
52/D2 **Kansas** (state), US
53/H3 **Kansas** (riv.), Ks,US
53/J3 **Kansas City,** Ks,US
53/J3 **Kansas City,** Mo,US
24/K4 **Kansk,** Rus.
62/G3 **Kanuku** (mts.), Guy.
30/D3 **Kaohsiung,** Tai.
42/B4 **Kaokoveld,** Namb.
42/B4 **Kaokoveld** (mts.), Namb.
41/B5 **Kaolack,** Sen.
36/C4 **Kapuas** (riv.), Indo.
24/G2 **Kara** (sea), Rus.
24/F5 **Kara-Bogaz-Gol** (gulf), Trkm.
23/D5 **Karabük,** Turk.
33/J4 **Karachi,** Pak.
30/B2 **Karaganda,** Kaz.
25/S4 **Karaginskiy** (isl.), Rus.
32/F1 **Karaj,** Iran
33/K1 **Karakoram** (mts.), Asia
28/E2 **Karakorum** (ruins), Mong.
24/F5 **Karakumy** (des.), Trkm.
25/S4 **Karanginskiy** (bay), Rus.
42/E4 **Kariba** (lake), Afr.
36/C4 **Karimata** (str.), Indo.
41/L8 **Karisimbi** (vol.), Zaire
41/Q6 **Karkaar** (mts.), Som.
23/D4 **Karkinitsk** (gulf), Ukr.
19/H4 **Karlovy Vary,** Czh.
18/G4 **Karlsruhe,** Ger.
23/C6 **Kárpathos** (isl.), Gre.
23/F5 **Kars,** Turk.
42/C1 **Kasai** (riv.), Zaire
32/F2 **Kashan,** Iran
30/C4 **Kashi** (Kashgar), China
41/N4 **Kassala,** Sudan
18/G4 **Kassel,** Ger.
33/K2 **Kasūr,** Pak.
55/G2 **Katahdin** (mt.), Me,US
42/D2 **Katanga** (reg.), Zaire
34/E2 **Kathmandu** (cap.), Nepal
19/J4 **Katowice,** Pol.
40/G5 **Katsina,** Nga.
22/D4 **Kattegat** (str.), Eur.
47/K2 **Kauai** (isl.), Hi,US
42/C5 **Kaukaveld,** Namb.
19/K3 **Kaunas,** Lith.
29/M4 **Kawasaki,** Japan
23/E6 **Kayseri,** Turk.
31/B2 **Kazakh** (uplands), Kaz.
24/G5 **Kazakhstan**
23/G2 **Kazan',** Rus.
53/H2 **Kearney,** Ne,US
21/J5 **Kecskemét,** Hun.
36/D5 **Kediri,** Indo.
30/D2 **Keelung,** Tai.
55/F3 **Keene,** NH,US
36/B3 **Kelang,** Malay.
50/D3 **Kelowna,** BC,Can
50/C4 **Kelso,** Wa,US
24/J4 **Kemerovo,** Rus.
57/H5 **Kendall,** Fl,US
40/D1 **Kenitra,** Mor.
57/F4 **Kenner,** La,US
50/D4 **Kennewick,** Wa,US
54/C3 **Kenosha,** Wi,US
54/D3 **Kent,** Oh,US
54/B4 **Kentucky** (lake), US
54/C4 **Kentucky** (state), US
39/F4 **Kenya**
41/M8 **Kenya** (Batian) (mt.), Kenya
53/K2 **Keokuk,** Ia,US
23/E4 **Kerch,** Ukr.
21/H4 **Kérkira** (Corfu) (isl.), Gre.
46/G7 **Kermadec** (isls.), NZ
33/G2 **Kerman,** Iran
52/D4 **Kerrville,** Tx,US
24/J4 **Ket'** (riv.), Rus.
24/K2 **Keta** (riv.), Rus.
49/D4 **Ketchikan,** Ak,US
54/C4 **Kettering,** Oh,US
54/B2 **Keweenaw** (pen.), Mi,US
54/C2 **Keweenaw** (pt.), Mi,US
57/H5 **Key West,** Fl,US
29/M2 **Khabarovsk,** Rus.
21/J3 **Khalkhidhikhi** (pen.), Gre.
21/J4 **Khalkís,** Gre.
32/D5 **Khamīs Mushayţ,** SAr.
29/L3 **Khanka** (lake), China, Rus.
24/G3 **Khanty-Mansiysk,** Rus.
34/E3 **Kharagpur,** India
23/E3 **Khar'kov,** Ukr.
41/M4 **Khartoum** (cap.), Sudan
41/M4 **Khartoum North,** Sudan
25/L2 **Khatanga** (gulf), Rus.
25/L2 **Khatanga** (riv.), Rus.
23/D4 **Kherson,** Ukr.
21/K4 **Khíos** (isl.), Gre.
21/C4 **Khmel'nitskiy,** Ukr.
23/F3 **Khopër** (riv.), Rus.
32/E2 **Khorramabad,** Iran
32/E2 **Khorramshahr,** Iran
35/H4 **Kho Sawai** (plat.), Thai.
34/E3 **Khulna,** Bang.
33/J3 **Khuzdār,** Pak.
23/G6 **Khvoy,** Iran
33/K2 **Khyber** (pass), Asia
40/F5 **Kianji** (lake), Nga.
18/G3 **Kiel,** Ger.
19/K4 **Kielce,** Pol.
23/D3 **Kiev** (cap.), Ukr.

64/B5 Quilán (cape), Chile
20/B1 Quimper, Fr.
54/B4 Quincy, Il,US
55/G3 Quincy, Ma,US
35/J5 Qui Nhon, Viet.
62/C4 Quito (cap.), Ecu.
30/C2 Quzhou, China

R

40/D1 Rabat (cap.), Mor.
46/E5 Rabaul, PNG
41/K3 Rabyanāh, Sahra' (des.), Libya
49/M5 Race (cape), Nf,Can
54/C3 Racine, Wi,US
19/K4 Radom, Pol.
21/H4 Ragusa, It.
33/K3 Rahīmyār Khān, Pak.
50/C4 Rainier (mt.), Wa,US
51/K3 Rainy (lake), NAm.
34/D3 Raipur, India
34/D4 Rajahmundry, India
36/D3 Rajang (riv.), Malay.
34/B3 Rajkot, India
34/E3 Rājshāhi, Bang.
33/K1 Rakaposhi (mtn.), Pak.
57/J3 Raleigh (cap.), NC,US
63/K6 Ramalho (mts.), Braz.
18/E4 Ramsgate, Eng,UK
34/E3 Ranchi, India
35/G4 Rangoon (cap.), Burma
54/B3 Rantoul, Il,US
47/L7 Rapa (isl.), FrPol.
51/H4 Rapid City, SD,US
54/E4 Rappahannock (riv.), Va,US
47/J7 Rarotonga (isl.), Cook Is.
64/D5 Rasa (pt.), Arg.
41/N5 Ras Dashen Terara (mt.), Eth.
32/E1 Rasht, Iran
32/F3 Ra's Tannūrah (cape), SAr.
45/H6 Raupehu (mtn.), NZ
34/D3 Raurkela, India
21/G2 Ravenna, It.
21/F2 Ravensburg, Ger.
33/K2 Ravi (riv.), Asia
33/K2 Rawalpindi, Pak.
50/G5 Rawlins, Wy,US
55/K2 Ray (cape), Nf,Can
21/K3 Razgrad, Bul.
18/D4 Reading, Eng,UK
54/F3 Reading, Pa,US
62/E7 Real (mts.), Bol.
63/M5 Recife, Braz.
32/C4 Red (sea)
27/K7 Red (riv.), Asia
53/J5 Red (riv.), US
50/E2 Red Deer, Ab,Can
50/F3 Red Deer (riv.), Ab,Can
52/B2 Redding, Ca,US
51/J4 Red River of the North (riv.), US
41/N3 Red Sea (hills), Sudan
52/A2 Redwood Nat'l Pk., Ca,US
18/C3 Ree (lake), Ire.
18/G4 Regensburg, Ger.
21/G4 Reggio di Calabria, It.
21/F2 Reggio nell'Emilia, It.
51/G3 Regina (cap.), Sk,Can
20/E1 Reims, Fr.
64/A7 Reina Adelaida (arch.), Chile
49/G4 Reindeer (lake), Can.
54/E2 Renfrew, On,Can
20/C1 Rennes, Fr.
52/C3 Reno, Nv,US
28/H4 Renqiu, China
53/H2 Republican (riv.), US
64/E2 Resistencia, Arg.
21/J2 Reşiţa, Rom.
21/J2 Retrezap Nat'l Park, Rom.
15/M7 Réunion, Fr.
18/G4 Reutlingen, Ger.
50/D3 Revelstoke, BC,Can
49/F8 Revillagigedo (isls.), Mex.
50/F5 Rexburg, Id,US
22/N7 Reykjavík (cap.), Ice.
58/B2 Reynosa, Mex.
18/F3 Rhine (riv.), Eur.
55/G3 Rhode Island (state), US
23/C6 Rhodes (isl.), Gre.
23/C6 Rhodes (Ródhos), Gre.
18/D4 Rhondda, Wal,UK
20/E2 Rhône (riv.), Eur.
18/C2 Rhum (isl.), Sc,UK
36/B3 Riau (arch.), Indo.
63/J8 Ribeirão Preto, Braz.
50/D4 Richland, Wa,US
54/C4 Richmond, In,US
54/C4 Richmond, Ky,US
54/E4 Richmond (cap.), Va,US
51/H3 Riding Mtn. Nat'l Pk., Mb,Can
40/E1 Rif, Er (mts.), Mor.
19/L2 Riga (cap.), Lat.
19/K2 Riga (gulf), Lat.
33/H2 Rīgestan (des.), Afg.
21/G2 Rijeka, Cro.
21/K2 Rîmimicu Vîlcea, Rom.
21/G2 Rimini, It.
55/G1 Rimouski, Qu,Can
62/C5 Río Abiseo Nat'l Park, Peru
62/E5 Rio Branco, Braz.
63/J8 Rio Claro, Braz.
64/D3 Río Cuarto, Arg.
63/K8 Rio de Janeiro, Braz.
56/C4 Rio Grande (riv.), NAm.
62/F4 Rio Jaú Nat'l Park, Braz.
64/E3 Río Negro (res.), Uru.
62/D2 Ritacuba (mtn.), Col.
45/D4 Riverina (reg.), Austl.
52/C4 Riverside, Ca,US
57/H5 Riviera Beach, Fl,US
55/G2 Rivière-du-Loup, Qu,Can
32/E4 Riyadh (cap.), SAr.
23/F5 Rize, Turk.
29/H4 Rizhao, China
59/J4 Road Town (cap.), BVI
54/E4 Roanoke, Va,US
57/J2 Roanoke Rapids, NC,US
55/F1 Roberval, Qu,Can
45/A3 Robinson (ranges), Austl.
51/K4 Rochester, Mn,US
55/G3 Rochester, NH,US
54/E3 Rochester, NY,US
54/B3 Rockford, Il,US
45/E2 Rockhampton, Austl.
57/H3 Rock Hill, SC,US
54/B3 Rock Island, Il,US
50/F5 Rock Springs, Wy,US
49/E4 Rocky (mts.), NAm.
57/J3 Rocky Mount, NC,US
50/E2 Rocky Mountain House, Ab,Can
53/F2 Rocky Mountain Nat'l Pk., Co,US
53/J3 Rogers, Ar,US
21/J2 Romania
21/G3 Rome (cap.), It.
57/G3 Rome, Ga,US
54/F3 Rome, NY,US
63/H6 Roncador (mts.), Braz.
43/W Ronne Ice Shelf, Ant.
63/H6 Ronuro (riv.), Braz.
43/N Roosevelt (isl.), Ant.
62/F6 Roosevelt (riv.), Braz.
62/F2 Roraima (mtn.), Guy.
64/D3 Rosario, Arg.
59/J4 Roseau (cap.), Dom.
50/C5 Roseburg, Or,US
18/H5 Rosenheim, Ger.
43/P Ross (sea), Ant.
43/P Ross Ice Shelf, Ant.
18/H3 Rostock, Ger.
23/E4 Rostov, Rus.
53/F4 Roswell, NM,US
18/D3 Rotherham, Eng,UK
18/F4 Rotterdam, Neth.
46/G6 Rotuma (isl.), Fiji
20/D1 Rouen, Fr.
54/E1 Rouyn-Noranda, Qu,Can
23/C3 Rovno, Ukr.
52/D2 Roy, Ut,US
42/F2 Ruaha Nat'l Park, Tanz.
32/E5 Rub' al Khali (des.), Asia
24/G4 Rudnyy, Kaz.
42/G2 Rufiji (riv.), Tanz.
19/H3 Rügen (isl.), Ger.
42/F2 Rukwa (lake), Tanz.
59/G3 Rum (cay), Bahm.
54/E1 Rupert (riv.), Qu,Can
21/K3 Ruse, Bulg.
24/H3 Russia
23/G5 Rustavi, Geo.
56/E3 Ruston, La,US
55/F3 Rutland, Vt,US
42/G3 Ruvuma (riv.), Tanz.
42/E1 Rwanda
23/E3 Ryazan', Rus.
23/E2 Rybinsk, Rus.
23/E2 Rybinsk (res.), Rus.
19/M5 Rybnitsa, Mol.
23/G4 Ryn-Peski (des.), Kaz.
46/B2 Ryukyu (isls.), Japan
19/K4 Rzeszów, Pol.

S

50/C3 Saanich, BC,Can
18/F4 Saarbrücken, Ger.
19/K2 Saaremaa (isl.), Est.
21/H2 Šabac, Yugo.
20/D3 Sabadell, Sp.
37/E2 Sabah (reg.), Malay.
56/E4 Sabine (riv.), US
55/H3 Sable (cape), NS,Can
55/J3 Sable (isl.), NS,Can
33/G1 Sabzevar, Iran
55/H2 Sackville, NB,Can
52/B3 Sacramento (cap.), Ca,US
52/B2 Sacramento (riv.), Ca,US
53/F4 Sacramento (mts.), NM,US
40/H1 Safāqis (Sfax), Tun.
40/D1 Safi, Mor.
33/H2 Safīd (mts.), Afg.
29/L5 Saga, Japan
54/D3 Saginaw, Mi,US
55/G1 Saguenay (riv.), Qu,Can
40/G3 Sahara (des.), Afr.
33/L3 Sahāranpur, India
33/K2 Sāhīwāl, Pak.
35/J5 Saigon (Ho Chi Minh City), Viet.
50/E2 St. Albert, Ab,Can
57/H4 St. Augustine, Fl,US
54/E3 St. Catharines, On,Can
53/K3 St. Charles, Mo,US
51/K4 St. Cloud, Mn,US
51/K4 St. Croix (riv.), US
59/H4 St. Croix (isl.), USVI
54/F2 Ste-Agathe-des-Monts, Qu,Can
55/G2 Ste-Foy, Qu,Can
20/E2 St-Étienne, Fr.
55/K1 St. George (cape), Nf,Can
18/C4 St. George's (chan.), Eur.
59/J5 St. George's (cap.), Gren.
42/C7 St. Helena (bay), SAfr.
14/J6 St. Helena & Dependencies, UK
50/C4 St. Helens (mt.), Wa,US
18/D4 St. Helier (cap.), Jersey, Chl.,UK
55/F2 St-Hyacinthe, Qu,Can
55/F1 St-Jean (lake), Qu,Can
55/F2 St-Jérôme, Qu,Can
55/H2 St. John, NB,Can
55/H2 St. John (riv.), NAm.
59/J4 St. Johns (cap.), Anti.
55/L2 St. John's (cap.), Nf,Can
53/J3 St. Joseph, Mo,US
59/J4 St. Kitts (isl.), StK.
59/J4 St. Kitts & Nevis
63/H2 Saint-Laurent-du-Maroni, FrG.
55/J1 St. Lawrence (gulf), Can.
55/G1 St. Lawrence (riv.), NAm.
49/A3 St. Lawrence (isl.), Ak,US
53/K3 St. Louis, Mo,US
59/J5 St. Lucia
20/C1 Saint-Malo, Fr.
20/C1 Saint-Malo (gulf), Fr.
59/J4 Saint Martin (isl.), Fr.
55/F2 St-Maurice (riv.), Qu,Can
20/C2 St-Nazaire, Fr.
51/K4 St. Paul (cap.), Mn,US
18/D4 St. Peter Port (cap.), Guernsey, Chl.,UK
23/D2 St. Petersburg, Rus.
57/H5 St. Petersburg, Fl,US
55/K2 St. Pierre & Miquelon, Fr.
57/H4 St. Simons (isl.), Ga,US
55/H2 St. Stephen, NB,Can
54/D3 St. Thomas, On,Can
59/H4 St. Thomas (isl.), USVI
59/J5 St. Vincent & the Grenadines
46/D3 Saipan (isl.), NMar.
29/M5 Sakai, Japan
51/H4 Sakakawea (lake), ND,US
23/D5 Sakarya (riv.), Turk.
25/Q4 Sakhalin (gulf), Rus.
25/Q4 Sakhalin (isl.), Rus.
30/D3 Sakishima (isls.), Japan
64/D2 Salado (riv.), Arg.
20/B3 Salamanca, Sp.
14/D7 Sala y Gómez (isl.), Chile
40/D1 Salé, Mor.
24/G3 Salekhard, Rus.
34/C5 Salem, India
55/G3 Salem, NH,US
50/C4 Salem (cap.), Or,US
54/D4 Salem, Va,US
21/G3 Salerno, It.
53/H3 Salina, Ks,US
52/B3 Salinas, Ca,US
18/D4 Salisbury, Eng,UK
54/F4 Salisbury, Md,US
50/E4 Salmon (riv.), Id,US
50/E4 Salmon River (mts.), Id,US
41/K8 Salonga Nat'l Park, Zaire
64/C1 Salta, Arg.
58/A2 Saltillo, Mex.
52/E2 Salt Lake City (cap.), Ut,US
64/E3 Salto Grande (res.), Arg., Uru.
52/C4 Salton Sea (lake), Ca,US
57/H3 Saluda (riv.), SC,US
63/H2 Salut (isls.), FrG.
63/L6 Salvador, Braz.
27/J8 Salween (riv.), Asia
21/G2 Salzburg, Aus.
18/G3 Salzgitter, Ger.
30/E5 Samar (isl.), Phil.
23/H3 Samara, Rus.
37/E4 Samarinda, Indo.
24/G6 Samarkand, Uzb.
36/C3 Sambas, Indo.
21/K4 Sámos (isl.), Gre.
21/K3 Samothráki (isl.), Gre.
23/E5 Samsun, Turk.
32/D5 Sanaa (San'a) (cap.), Yem.
58/E5 San Andrés (isl.), Col.
56/C4 San Angelo, Tx,US
56/D4 San Antonio, Tx,US
52/C4 San Bernardino, Ca,US
64/B3 San Bernardo, Chile
52/C4 San Clemente (isl.), Ca,US
46/F6 San Cristobal (isl.), Sol.
62/D2 San Cristóbal, Ven.
52/C4 San Diego, Ca,US
54/D3 Sandusky, Oh,US
52/E2 Sandy, Ut,US
57/G3 Sandy Springs, Ga,US
57/H4 Sanford, Fl,US
55/G3 Sanford, Me,US
57/J3 Sanford, NC,US
52/B3 San Francisco, Ca,US
62/C4 Sangay Nat'l Park, Ecu.
34/B4 Sāngli, India
53/F3 Sangre de Cristo (mts.), US
52/B3 San Joaquin (val.), Ca,US
64/C6 San Jorge (gulf), Arg.
58/E6 San José (cap.), CR
52/B3 San Jose, Ca,US
62/J8 San José dos Campos, Braz.
64/C3 San Juan, Arg.
59/H4 San Juan (cap.), PR
52/E3 San Juan (riv.), US
21/F2 Sankt Gallen, Swi.
62/B4 San Lorenzo (cape), Ecu.
59/N9 San Lucas (cape), Mex.
52/B4 San Luis Obispo, Ca,US
58/A3 San Luis Potosí, Mex.
56/D4 San Marcos, Tx,US
21/G3 San Marino
52/B3 San Mateo, Ca,US
64/D5 San Matías (gulf), Arg.
62/F6 San Miguel (riv.), Bol.
58/D5 San Miguel, ESal.
64/C2 San Miguel de Tucumán, Arg.
52/C4 San Nicolas (isl.), Ca,US
58/A2 San Nicolás de los Garzas, Mex.
25/P2 Sannikova (str.), Rus.
64/C1 San Pedro (vol.), Chile
58/D4 San Pedro Sula, Hon.
62/C3 Sanquianga Nat'l Park, Col.
20/E3 San Remo, It.
59/G3 San Salvador (isl.), Bahm.
58/D5 San Salvador (cap.), ESal.
64/C1 San Salvador de Jujuy, Arg.
20/C3 San Sebastián, Sp.
58/D5 Santa Ana, ESal.
52/C4 Santa Ana, Ca,US
52/C4 Santa Barbara, Ca,US
52/C4 Santa Catalina (isl.), Ca,US
64/G2 Santa Catarina (isl.), Braz.
59/E3 Santa Clara, Cuba
62/F7 Santa Cruz, Bol.
40/B2 Santa Cruz (isls.), Sol.
52/B3 Santa Cruz, Ca,US
40/B2 Santa Cruz de Tenerife, Sp.
64/D3 Santa Fe, Arg.
53/F4 Santa Fe (cap.), NM,US
64/B7 Santa Inés (isl.), Chile
64/F2 Santa Maria, Braz.
52/B4 Santa Maria, Ca,US
62/D1 Santa Marta, Col.
20/C3 Santander, Sp.
20/F3 Sant'Antioco (isl.), It.
63/H4 Santarém, Braz.
52/B3 Santa Rosa, Ca,US
57/J3 Santee (riv.), SC,US
64/B3 Santiago (cap.), Chile
59/G4 Santiago, DRep.
56/C4 Santiago (mts.), Tx,US
20/A3 Santiago de Compostela, Sp.
59/F4 Santiago de Cuba, Cuba
64/D2 Santiago del Estero, Arg.
64/G1 Santo André, Braz.
59/H4 Santo Domingo (cap.), DRep.
62/B3 Santo Domingo de los Colorados, Ecu.
64/G1 Santos, Braz.
64/B6 San Valentín (mtn.), Chile
63/J8 São Carlos, Braz.
64/G2 São Francisco (isl.), Braz.
63/L5 São Francisco (riv.), Braz.
63/K4 São João (isls.), Braz.
62/F5 São João (mts.), Braz.
63/K8 São João del Rei, Braz.
63/J8 São José do Rio Preto, Braz.
63/J8 São José dos Campos, Braz.
63/G7 São Lourenço (riv.), Braz.
63/K4 São Luís, Braz.
63/K4 São Marcos (bay), Braz.
20/E2 Saône (riv.), Fr.
64/G1 São Paulo, Braz.
63/M5 São Roque (cape), Braz.
63/K8 São Tomé (cape), Braz.
40/G7 São Tomé (cap.), SaoT.
40/F7 São Tomé and Príncipe
20/A4 São Vincent (cape), Port.
29/N3 Sapporo, Japan
20/C3 Saragossa, Sp.
21/H3 Sarajevo (cap.), Bosn.
23/G3 Saransk, Rus.
23/H2 Sarapul, Rus.
57/H5 Sarasota, Fl,US
54/F3 Saratoga Springs, NY,US
23/G3 Saratov, Rus.
36/D3 Sarawak (reg.), Malay.
21/F3 Sardinia (isl.), It.
33/K2 Sargodha, Pak.
32/F1 Sāri, Iran
54/D3 Sarnia, On,Can
29/K5 Sasebo, Japan
50/G2 Saskatchewan (prov.), Can.
51/G2 Saskatchewan (riv.), Can.
50/G3 Saskatoon, Sk,Can
20/F3 Sassari, It.
34/C3 Satpura (range), India
21/J2 Satu Mare, Rom.
32/D4 Saudi Arabia
54/C2 Sault Ste. Marie, On,Can
54/C2 Sault Ste. Marie, Mi,US
21/H2 Sava (riv.), Eur.
47/R9 Savai'i (isl.), WSam.
57/H3 Savannah (riv.), US
57/H3 Savannah, Ga,US
35/H4 Savannaket, Laos
42/F5 Save (riv.), Moz.
20/F2 Savona, It.
37/F5 Savu (sea), Indo.
52/F3 Sawatch (range), Co,US
41/M2 Sawhāj, Egypt
52/D1 Sawtooth (mts.), Id,US
18/D3 Scarborough, Eng,UK
21/F2 Schaffhausen, Swi.
54/F3 Schenectady, NY,US
18/G4 Schwäbische Alb (range), Ger.
18/G4 Schweinfurt, Ger.
18/G3 Schwerin, Ger.
18/C4 Scilly (isls.), Eng,UK
54/D4 Scioto (riv.), Oh,US
43/W Scotia (sea), Ant.
18/C2 Scotland, UK
52/G2 Scottsbluff, Ne,US
57/G3 Scottsboro, Al,US
52/E4 Scottsdale, Az,US
54/F3 Scranton, Pa,US
21/H3 Scutari (lake), Eur.
50/C4 Seattle, Wa,US
62/B5 Sechura (bay), Peru
62/B5 Sechura (des.), Peru
53/J3 Sedalia, Mo,US
20/B3 Segovia, Sp.
20/D1 Seine (riv.), Fr.
40/E7 Sekondi, Gha.
50/D3 Selkirk (mts.), BC,Can
51/J3 Selkirk, Mb,Can
57/G3 Selma, Al,US
62/E5 Selvas (for.), Braz.
36/D5 Semarang, Indo.
31/D1 Semipalatinsk, Kaz.
40/B5 Senegal
40/B4 Senegal (riv.), Afr.
29/K4 Seoul (cap.), SKor.
55/H1 Sept-Îles, Qu,Can
52/C3 Sequoia Nat'l Pk., Ca,US
36/C3 Serasan (str.), Malay.
42/F1 Serengeti (plain), Tanz.
42/F1 Serengeti Nat'l Park, Kenya, Tanz.
63/H5 Seringa (mts.), Braz.
24/G4 Serov, Rus.
23/E3 Serpukhov, Rus.
63/K5 Serra da Capivara Nat'l Park, Braz.
62/E3 Serranía de la Neblina Nat'l Park, Ven.
40/G1 Sétif, Alg.
20/A4 Setúbal, Port.
20/A4 Setúbal (bay), Port.
23/G5 Sevan (lake), Arm.
23/E5 Sevastopol', Ukr.
21/J2 Severnaya Zemlya (isls.), Rus.
17/H2 Severodvinsk, Rus.
52/D3 Sevier (riv.), Ut,US
20/B4 Seville, Sp.
49/C3 Seward, Ak,US
15/M6 Seychelles
23/E6 Seyhan (riv.), Turk.
18/F3 's Gravenhage (The Hague) (cap.), Neth.
34/C2 Shahjahanpur, India
35/G3 Shan (plat.), Burma
29/J4 Shandong (pen.), China
29/J5 Shanghai, China
30/C2 Shangrao, China
18/B3 Shannon (riv.), Ire.
25/P4 Shantar (isls.), Rus.
30/B3 Shaoguan, China
30/D2 Shaoxing, China
30/B2 Shaoyang, China
54/D3 Sharon, Pa,US
52/B2 Shasta (lake), Ca,US
52/B2 Shasta (mt.), Ca,US
32/E2 Shatt-al-'Arab (riv.), Asia
40/G1 Shaţţ al Jarīd (depr.), Tun.
55/F2 Shawinigan, Qu,Can
53/H4 Shawnee, Ok,US
54/B3 Sheboygan, Wi,US
18/D3 Sheffield, Eng,UK
33/K2 Shekhūpura, Pak.
25/S2 Shelagskiy (cape), Rus.
57/H3 Shelby, NC,US
25/R3 Shelekhov (gulf), Rus.
54/E4 Shenandoah Nat'l Pk., Va,US
29/J3 Shenyang (Mukden), China
55/G2 Sherbrooke, Qu,Can
50/G4 Sheridan, Wy,US
56/D3 Sherman, Tx,US
18/F3 's Hertogenbosch, Neth.
50/E2 Sherwood Park, Ab,Can
18/D1 Shetland (isls.), Sc,UK
24/F5 Shevchenko, Kaz.
51/J4 Sheyenne (riv.), ND,US
31/E3 Shihezi, China
28/G4 Shijiazhuang, China
29/L5 Shikoku (isl.), Japan
35/F2 Shillong, India
29/M5 Shimizu, Japan
29/L5 Shimonoseki, Japan
32/F3 Shiraz, Iran
30/B2 Shishou, China
28/G5 Shiyan, China
28/F4 Shizuishan, China
29/M5 Shizuoka, Japan
21/H3 Shkodër, Alb.
34/C4 Sholapur, India
56/E3 Shreveport, La,US
29/L2 Shuangyashan, China
32/B2 Shubrā al Khaymah, Egypt
21/K3 Shumen, Bul.
33/H2 Siāh (mts.), Afg.
33/K2 Sialkot, Pak.
19/K3 Šiauliai, Lith.
24/K3 Siberia (reg.), Rus.
21/K2 Sibiu, Rom.
30/D5 Sibuyan (sea), Phil.
21/G4 Sicily (isl.), It.
40/E1 Sidi Bel-Abbès, Alg.
40/K1 Sidra (gulf), Libya
18/G4 Siegen, Ger.
62/D3 Sierra de la Macarena Nat'l Park, Col.
40/C6 Sierra Leone
52/C3 Sierra Nevada (mts.), US
62/D2 Sierra Nevada Nat'l Park, Ven.
52/E5 Sierra Vista, Az,US
29/M2 Sikhote-Alin' (mts.), Rus.
34/E2 Sikkim (state), India
19/H4 Silesia (reg.), Pol.
34/E2 Silīguri, India
23/G3 Simbirsk, Rus.
54/D3 Simcoe, On,Can
54/E2 Simcoe (lake), On,Can
41/N5 Simēn (mts.), Eth.
23/D5 Simferopol', Ukr.
45/C3 Simpson (des.), Austl.
32/B3 Sinai (pen.), Egypt
33/J3 Sind (reg.), Pak.
36/B3 Singapore
36/B3 Singapore (cap.), Sing.
36/C3 Singkawang, Indo.
23/E5 Sinop, Turk.
59/J4 Sint Maarten (isl.), NAnt.
29/J3 Sinŭiju, NKor.
42/D4 Sioma Ngwezi Nat'l Park, Zam.
53/H2 Sioux City, Ia,US
51/J5 Sioux Falls, SD,US
29/J3 Siping, China
21/G4 Siracusa (Syracuse), It.
21/K2 Siret (riv.), Rom.
35/F3 Sitākunda, Bang.
49/D4 Sitka, Ak,US
23/E6 Sivas, Turk.
41/L2 Siwah (oasis), Egypt
34/D2 Siwalik (range), India, Nepal
22/D4 Skagerrak (str.), Eur.
41/G1 Skikda, Alg.
21/K4 Skíros (isl.), Gre.
21/J3 Skopje (cap.), Macd.
18/C2 Skye (isl.), Sc,UK
49/F4 Slave (riv.), Can.
21/H2 Slavonski Brod, Cro.
57/F4 Slidell, La,US
18/B3 Sligo, Ire.
21/K3 Sliven, Bul.
19/J4 Slovakia
21/G2 Slovenia
19/J3 Słupsk, Pol.
21/J2 Smederevo, Yugo.
50/B2 Smithers, BC,Can
54/E2 Smiths Falls, On,Can
53/G3 Smoky Hill (riv.), Ks,US
23/D3 Smolensk, Rus.
57/G3 Smyrna, Ga,US
50/D5 Snake (riv.), US
18/C3 Snowdon (mt.), Wal,UK
63/K6 Sobradinho (res.), Braz.
23/E5 Sochi, Rus.
37/K6 Society (isls.), FrPol.
27/E8 Socotra (isl.), Yem.
21/J3 Sofia (cap.), Bulg.
62/C1 Soledad, Col.
62/E4 Solimões (Amazon) (riv.), Braz.
46/E5 Solomon (sea)
46/E6 Solomon Islands
18/C3 Solway (firth), UK
41/Q6 Somalia
49/H2 Somerset (isl.), NW,Can
20/D1 Somme (riv.), Fr.
29/K2 Songhua (riv.), China
35/H6 Songkhla, Thai.
55/F2 Sorel, Qu,Can
63/K8 Sorocaba, Braz.
37/H4 Sorong, Indo.
19/J4 Sosnowiec, Pol.
55/J2 Souris, PE,Can
51/H3 Souris (riv.), NAm.
45/H7 South (isl.), NZ
42/D6 South Africa
61/* South America
49/J3 Southampton (isl.), NW,Can
18/D4 Southampton, Eng,UK
45/C3 South Australia (state), Austl.
54/C3 South Bend, In,US
55/F2 South Burlington, Vt,US
57/H3 South Carolina (state), US
27/L8 South China (sea), Asia
51/H4 South Dakota (state), US
45/G7 Southern Alps (mts.), NZ
45/B2 Southesk Tablelands (plat.), Austl.
43/X South Georgia (isl.), Ant.
29/K4 South Korea
52/C3 South Lake Tahoe, Ca,US
43/W South Orkney (isls.), Ant.
23/F5 South Ossetia (reg.), Geo.
53/G2 South Platte (riv.), US
43/A South Pole
43/Y South Sandwich (isl.), Ant.
50/F3 South Saskatchewan (riv.), Can.
34/E3 South Suburban, India
42/E6 Soweto, SAfr.
20/B3 Spain
59/F4 Spanish Town, Jam.
52/C3 Sparks, Nv,US
57/H3 Spartanburg, SC,US
21/J4 Sparta (Spárti), Gre.
45/C4 Spencer (gulf), Austl.
24/B2 Spitsbergen (isl.), Nor.
21/H3 Split, Cro.
50/D4 Spokane, Wa,US
30/B5 Spratly (isls.)
19/H4 Spree (riv.), Ger.
53/J3 Springdale, Ar,US
54/B4 Springfield (cap.), Il,US
54/E3 Springfield, Ma,US
53/J3 Springfield, Mo,US
54/D4 Springfield, Oh,US
50/C4 Springfield, Or,US
54/F3 Springfield, Vt,US
55/H2 Springhill, NS,Can
50/C3 Squamish, BC,Can
33/K3 Sri Gangānagar, India
34/D6 Sri Lanka
33/K2 Srinagar, India
23/E4 Stakhanov, Ukr.
54/F3 Stamford, Ct,US
64/E7 Stanley (cap.), Falk.
41/L8 Stanley (falls), Zaire
25/N4 Stanovoy (range), Rus.
21/K3 Stara Zagora, Bulg.
57/F3 Starkville, Ms,US
23/E3 Staryy Oskol, Rus.
54/E3 State College, Pa,US
57/H3 Statesboro, Ga,US
57/H3 Statesville, NC,US
54/E4 Staunton, Va,US
22/C4 Stavanger, Nor.
23/F5 Stavropol', Rus.
23/G6 Stepanakert, Azer.
53/G2 Sterling, Co,US
24/F4 Sterlitamak, Rus.
54/D3 Steubenville, Oh,US
54/B2 Stevens Point, Wi,US
45/G7 Stewart (isl.), NZ
53/H3 Stillwater, Ok,US
18/D2 Stirling, Sc,UK
22/F4 Stockholm (cap.), Swe.
18/D3 Stockport, Eng,UK
52/B3 Stockton, Ca,US
56/C4 Stockton (plat.), Tx,US
18/D3 Stoke-on-Trent, Eng,UK
25/P2 Stolbovoy (isl.), Rus.
55/Q9 Stoney Creek, On,Can
19/H3 Stralsund, Ger.
20/E1 Strasbourg, Fr.
54/D3 Stratford, On,Can
21/G4 Stromboli (isl.), It.
21/J3 Struma (riv.), Bul.
45/D3 Sturt (des.), Austl.
18/G4 Stuttgart, Ger.
53/K4 Stuttgart, Ar,US
62/E7 Sucre (cap.), Bol.
62/G5 Sucunduri (riv.), Braz.
63/H7 Sucuriú (riv.), Braz.
41/L5 Sudan
40/H5 Sudan (reg.), Afr.
54/D2 Sudbury, On,Can
19/H4 Sudeten (mts.), Eur.
32/B3 Suez, Egypt
32/B3 Suez (canal), Egypt
32/B3 Suez (gulf), Egypt
54/E4 Suffolk, Va,US
28/F1 Sühbaatar, Mong.
36/C5 Sukabumi, Indo.
23/F5 Sukhumi, Geo.
33/J3 Sukkur, Pak.
37/G4 Sula (isls.), Indo.
33/J3 Sulaimān (range), Pak.
37/E4 Sulawesi (Celebes) (isl.), Indo.
53/J5 Sulphur, La,US
37/E2 Sulu (sea), Asia
37/F3 Sulu (arch.), Phil.
36/B4 Sumatra (isl.), Indo.
37/E5 Sumba (isl.), Indo.
37/E5 Sumba (str.), Indo.
37/E5 Sumbawa (isl.), Indo.
23/K5 Sumgait, Azer.
55/J2 Summerside, PE,Can
57/H3 Sumter, SC,US
23/D3 Sumy, Ukr.
36/D4 Sunda (isls.), Indo.
36/B5 Sunda (str.), Indo.
18/D3 Sunderland, Eng,UK
25/P3 Suntar-Khayata (mts.), Rus.
54/C2 Superior (lake), NAm.
54/A2 Superior, Wi,US
23/G3 Sura (riv.), Rus.
36/D5 Surabaya, Indo.
36/D5 Surakarta, Indo.
34/B3 Surat, India
24/H3 Surgut, Rus.
63/G3 Suriname
50/C3 Surrey, BC,Can
40/H1 Sūsah, Tun.
54/E4 Susquehanna (riv.), US
46/G6 Suva (cap.), Fiji
57/H4 Suwannee (riv.), US
29/J5 Suzhou, China
24/B2 Svalbard (isls.), Nor.
24/G4 Sverdlovsk (Yekaterinburg), Rus.
49/G2 Sverdrup (isls.), NW,Can
25/P2 Svyatyy Nos (cape), Rus.
58/E4 Swan (Santanilla) (isls.), Hon.
18/C4 Swansea, Wal,UK
42/F6 Swaziland
22/E3 Sweden
56/C3 Sweetwater, Tx,US
50/F5 Sweetwater (riv.), Wy,US
50/G3 Swift Current, Sk,Can
18/D4 Swindon, Eng,UK
20/E2 Switzerland
45/E4 Sydney, Austl.
55/J2 Sydney, NS,Can
54/E3 Syracuse, NY,US
24/G5 Syrdar'ya (riv.), Kaz.
32/C1 Syria
32/C2 Syrian (des.), Asia
24/G3 Syzran', Rus.
19/H3 Szczecin, Pol.
21/J2 Szeged, Hun.
21/H2 Székesfehérvár, Hun.
21/H2 Szombathely, Hun.

T

63/K6 Tabatinga (mts.), Braz.
50/E3 Taber, Ab,Can
42/F2 Tabora, Tanz.
23/G6 Tabriz, Iran
47/K4 Tabuaeran (isl.), Kiri.
32/C3 Tabūk, SAr.
50/C4 Tacoma, Wa,US
62/D7 Tacora (vol.), Chile
40/H2 Tadrart (mts.), Afr.
29/K4 T'aebaek (mts.), NKor., SKor.
29/K4 Taegu, SKor.
29/K4 Taejŏn, SKor.
40/G3 Tafassasset, Ténéré du (reg.), Niger
23/E4 Taganrog, Rus.
63/J7 Taguatinga, Braz.
20/B4 Tagus (riv.), Eur.
47/L6 Tahiti (isl.), FrPol.
52/C3 Tahoe (lake), US
29/H4 Tai'an, China
30/D3 Taichung, Tai.
30/D3 Tainan, Tai.
21/J4 Tainaron, Ákra (cape), Gre.
30/D2 Taipei (cap.), Tai.
36/B3 Taiping, Malay.
30/D3 Taiwan (Rep. of China)
30/C3 Taiwan (str.), China, Tai.
28/G4 Taiyuan, China
32/D6 Ta'izz, Yem.
24/H6 Tajikistan
32/F1 Tajrīsh, Iran
58/C4 Tajumulco (vol.), Guat.
29/L5 Takamatsu, Japan
29/M4 Takaoka, Japan
45/H6 Takapuna, NZ
31/D4 Takla Makan (des.), China
40/E6 Takoradi, Gha.
37/G3 Taland (isls.), Indo.
64/B4 Talca, Chile
64/B4 Talcahuano, Chile
57/G3 Talladega, Al,US
57/G4 Tallahassee (cap.), Fl,US
19/L2 Tallinn (cap.), Est.
33/J1 Tāloqān, Afg.
40/E6 Tamale, Gha.
23/F3 Tambov, Rus.
57/H5 Tampa, Fl,US
22/G3 Tampere, Fin.
58/B3 Tampico, Mex.
41/N5 Tana (lake), Eth.
45/C2 Tanami (des.), Austl.
64/E4 Tandil, Arg.
35/G4 Tanem (range), Thai.
40/E3 Tanezrouft (des.), Afr.
42/G2 Tanga, Tanz.
42/F2 Tanganyika (lake), Afr.
31/E5 Tanggula (mts.), China
40/D1 Tangier, Mor.
29/H4 Tangshan, China
37/H5 Tanimbar (isls.), Indo.
36/C5 Tanjungkarang, Indo.
32/B2 Tanta, Egypt
42/F2 Tanzania
53/F3 Taos, NM,US